Contents

W9-BYM-238

Contents

Name _____

Strategy Workshop

As you listen to the story "The Pumpkin Box," by Angela Johnson, you will stop from time to time to do some activities on these practice pages. These activities will help you think about different strategies that can help you read better. After completing each activity, you will discuss what you've written with your classmates and talk about how to use these strategies.

Remember, strategies can help you become a better reader. Good readers

- use strategies whenever they read

- use different strategies before, during, and after reading

- think about how strategies will help them

Name _____

Strategy 1: Predict/Infer

Use this strategy before and during reading to help make predictions about what happens next or what you're going to learn.

Here's how to use the Predict/Infer Strategy:

1. Think about the title, the illustrations, and what you have read so far.
2. Tell what you think will happen next—or what you will learn. Thinking about what you already know on the topic may help.
3. Try to figure out things the author does not say directly.

Listen as your teacher begins "The Pumpkin Box." When your teacher stops, complete the activity to show that you understand how to predict what the pumpkin box is.

Think about the story and respond to the question below.

What do you think the pumpkin box is?

_____

_____

_____

_____

As you continue listening to the story, think about whether your prediction was right. You might want to change your prediction or write a new one below.

_____

_____

_____

_____

_____

Name _____

Strategy 2: Phonics/Decoding

Use this strategy during reading when you come across a word you don't know.

Here's how to use the Phonics/Decoding Strategy:

1. Look carefully at the word.
2. Look for word parts you know and think about the sounds for the letters.
3. Blend the sounds to read the words.
4. Ask yourself: Is this a word I know? Does it make sense in what I am reading?
5. If not, ask yourself: What else can I try? Should I look in a dictionary?

Listen as your teacher continues the story. When your teacher stops, use the Phonics/Decoding Strategy.

Now write down the steps you used to decode the word *munching*.

_____

_____

_____

_____

_____

_____

_____

_____

_____

Remember to use this strategy whenever you are reading and come across a word that you don't know.

Name _____

Strategy 3: Monitor/Clarify

Use this strategy during reading whenever you're confused about what you are reading.

Here's how to use the Monitor/Clarify Strategy:

- Ask yourself if what you're reading makes sense—or if you are learning what you need to learn.
- If you don't understand something, reread, use the illustrations, or read ahead to see if that helps.

Listen as your teacher continues the story. When your teacher stops, complete the activity to show that you understand how to figure out how the pumpkin box got underground.

Think about the pumpkin box and respond below.

1. Describe the pumpkin box.

_____

_____

_____

2. Can you tell from listening to the story how the pumpkin box got there? Why or why not?

_____

_____

_____

_____

3. How can you find out why the pumpkin box was buried in the ground?

_____

_____

_____

_____

Name _____

Strategy 4: Question

Use this strategy during and after reading to ask questions about important ideas in the story.

Here's how to use the Question Strategy:

- Ask yourself questions about important ideas in the story.
- Ask yourself if you can answer these questions.
- If you can't answer the questions, reread and look for answers in the text. Thinking about what you already know and what you've read in the story may help you.

Listen as your teacher continues the story. Then complete the activity to show that you understand how to ask yourself questions about important ideas in the story.

Think about the story and respond below.

Write a question you might ask yourself at this point in the story.

_____

_____

_____

_____

_____

_____

_____

_____

_____

If you can't answer your question now, think about it while you listen to the rest of the story.

Name _____

Strategy 5: Evaluate

Use this strategy during and after reading to help you form an opinion about what you read.

Here's how to use the Evaluate Strategy:

- Tell whether or not you think this story is entertaining and why.
- Is the writing clear and easy to understand?
- This is a realistic fiction story. Did the author make the characters believable and interesting?

Listen as your teacher continues the story. When your teacher stops, complete the activity to show that you are thinking of how you feel about what you are reading and why you feel that way.

Think about the story and respond below.

1. Tell whether or not you think this story is entertaining and why.

_____

_____

_____

_____

2. Is the writing clear and easy to understand?

_____

_____

_____

3. This is a realistic fiction story. Did the author make the characters interesting and believable?

_____

_____

_____

Name _____

Strategy 6: Summarize

Use this strategy after reading to summarize what you read.

Here's how to use the Summarize Strategy:
- Think about the characters.
- Think about where the story takes place.
- Think about the problem in the story and how the characters solve it.
- Think about what happens in the beginning, middle, and end of the story.

Think about the story you just listened to. Complete the activity to show that you understand how to identify important story parts that will help you summarize the story.

Think about the story and respond to the questions below:

1. Who is the main character?

_____

_____

2. Where does the story take place?

_____

_____

3. What is the problem and how is it resolved?

_____

_____

Now use this information to summarize the story for a partner.

Name _____

Nature's Fury

After reading each selection, complete the chart below and on the next page to show what you discovered.

	What is the setting or settings for the action or descriptions in the selection?	What dangers do people face in the selection?
Earthquake Terror		
Eye of the Storm		
Volcanoes		

Name _____

Nature's Fury

After reading each selection, complete the chart to show what you
discovered.

	What warnings or events happen before nature's fury occurs in the selection?	What did you learn about an example of nature's fury in the selection?
Earthquake Terror		
Eye of the Storm		
Volcanoes		

What advice would you give others about the different kinds of nature's
fury featured in this theme?

_____

_____

Name _____

A Scientist's Report

Use the words in the box to complete the scientist's report on the Magpie Island earthquake.

Vocabulary

shuddered

debris

undulating

fault

jolt

Earthquake Report

Magpie Island lies near the San Andreas

_____, so it was susceptible to

the recent earthquake. On a cloudless day, witnesses

reported hearing a sound like thunder and feeling a

_____ as the earth started to

shake. Next, the ground below their feet

_____ and heaved. Trees began

to fall with a forceful impact. As the earthquake reached

its peak, the ground began _____

in a continuous motion.

After the shaking stopped, people examined the

devastation that the earthquake had caused.

_____ lay everywhere. The

upheaval had struck a great blow to the island.

Name _____

Event Map

Record in this Event Map the main story events in the order in which they occurred.

Page 30

At first Moose listens. Then he barks and paces back and forth as if he senses _____

↓

Pages 30–31

After Jonathan puts the leash on Moose, they all slowly start to _____

↓

Pages 32–33

Jonathan and Abby hear a strange noise. At first Jonathan thinks it is thunder or hunters. Then suddenly he realizes they are _____

_____

↓

Page 35

Abby screams and falls. As Jonathan lunges forward, he tries to catch Abby. Then he shouts, _____

↓

Pages 36–37

Jonathan sees the huge redwood tree sway back and forth. Then _____

_____

Name _____

True or False?

Read each sentence. Write T if the sentence is true, or F if the sentence is false. If a sentence is false, correct it to make it true.

1. _____ Jonathan and Abby's parents had left the island to go grocery shopping.

   _____

2. _____ Moose became restless because he could feel the earthquake coming.

   _____

3. _____ Jonathan thought the first rumblings of the earthquake were distant thunder.

   _____

4. _____ Jonathan knew what to do because he had been in an earthquake before.

   _____

5. _____ When the giant redwood began to fall, Moose dragged Jonathan to safety.

   _____

6. _____ Jonathan and Abby found shelter in a large ditch.

   _____

7. _____ In a panic, Moose ran off and didn't come back.

   _____

8. _____ As quickly as it had begun, the earthquake stopped and the woods were silent.

   _____

Name _____

Mapping the Sequence

Read this passage. Then complete the activity on page 15.

Rapids Ahead!

Alison scanned the river nervously. She had already endured two sets of violent rapids. Each time, she had grasped the ropes of the raft so hard that her knuckles turned white. Luckily, the guide on her raft was strong and skilled. "Relax, Alison," Anushka had smiled when the trip had begun three hours earlier. "Rafting is a blast, once you get the hang of it."

During the first hour on the river, Anushka had taught Alison how to paddle on one side to make the raft go in the opposite direction. She had instructed Alison on what to do if the raft flipped or if she were tossed out. "Don't fight the current," Anushka had said. "Let it carry you downstream as you swim for the shore."

Six months earlier, when Alison's parents had proposed a whitewater rafting trip down the Snake River, Alison said, "No way." Her brother Zack was thrilled, though, so Alison's parents signed all four of them up for a seven-day run. So far, the trip was as bad as Alison had expected.

"Rapids ahead. Hold on!" Anushka said. Alison's stomach knotted as the raft pitched forward with the current. "Paddle left!" Anushka shouted. As Alison's paddle hit the water, the bow of the raft hit a boulder and shot into the air. Alison shut her eyes as icy water drenched her.

When she opened her eyes, Anushka was gone. In a panic, Alison scanned the rapids. "Anushka!" she screamed. Then she saw her. Anushka was making her way to shore, feet first, letting the current do the work. "It's up to me now," Alison said to herself. She paddled left, then right, steering between the rocks. She was amazed that she could control it. Left. Right. Left again. Now Anushka was on the bank, shouting directions over the roar of the river. Alison managed to nose the raft into an eddy and a moment later, onto the shore.

"Great job, Alison!" Anushka grinned. "You really kept your head out there!" Alison beamed. Maybe this trip would be all right after all.

14   Theme 1: **Nature's Fury**

Mapping the Sequence continued

**Write each story event from page 14 in the sequence
map below. Put the events in order.**

➤ Alison successfully guides the raft to shore.

➤ Anushka tells Alison to relax.

➤ The raft hits a boulder and Anushka falls overboard.

➤ Anushka teaches Alison how to steer the raft.

➤ Alison's parents suggest a raft trip on the Snake River.

↓

↓

↓

↓

**Now go back to the passage. Circle the words that helped you
understand the following:**

➤ when the family plans the trip

➤ when Anushka tells Alison that rafting is fun

➤ when Anushka teaches Alison some basic rafting techniques

➤ whether Anushka's spill occurs during the first, second, or third
   set of rapids that she and Alison encounter

Name _____

Getting to Base

Read the sentences. For each underlined word, identify the base word. Write the base word and the ending.

Example: shake + -ing

1. Magpie Island was a popular place for <u>hiking</u>. _____

2. Jonathan was nervous about staying in such an <u>isolated</u> place.

   _____

3. He thought it would be <u>safer</u> to go back to their trailer.

   _____

4. Jonathan and Abby followed the trail past blackberry <u>bushes</u>.

   _____

5. Neither of them had the <u>slightest</u> idea how the day would end.

   _____

6. Moose cocked his head and began <u>sniffing</u> the ground.

   _____

7. At first the earthquake was a <u>thunderous</u> noise in the distance.

   _____

8. Trees <u>swayed</u> all around Jonathan and Abby.

   _____

9. The ground began rising and falling like ocean <u>waves</u>.

   _____

10. Abby <u>cried</u> for Jonathan to come help her. _____

Name _____

Short Vowels

Remember that a short vowel sound is usually spelled by one vowel and followed by a consonant sound. This is the **short vowel pattern.** These vowels usually spell short vowel sounds:

/ă/ *a*   /ĕ/ *e*   /ĭ/ *i*   /ŏ/ *o*   /ŭ/ *u*

▶ The short vowel sounds in the starred words do not have the usual short vowel spelling patterns. The /ĕ/ sound is spelled *ea* in *breath* and *deaf*. The /ŭ/ sound is spelled *ou* in *tough* and *rough*.

Write each Spelling Word under its vowel sound.

1. bunk
2. staff
3. dock
4. slept
5. mist
6. bunch
7. swift
8. stuck
9. breath*
10. tough*
11. fond
12. crush
13. grasp
14. dwell
15. fund
16. ditch
17. split
18. swept
19. deaf*
20. rough*

/ă/ Sound

_____

_____

/ĕ/ Sound

_____

_____

_____

/ĭ/ Sound

_____

_____

_____

/ŏ/ Sound

_____

_____

/ŭ/ Sound

_____

_____

_____

_____

_____

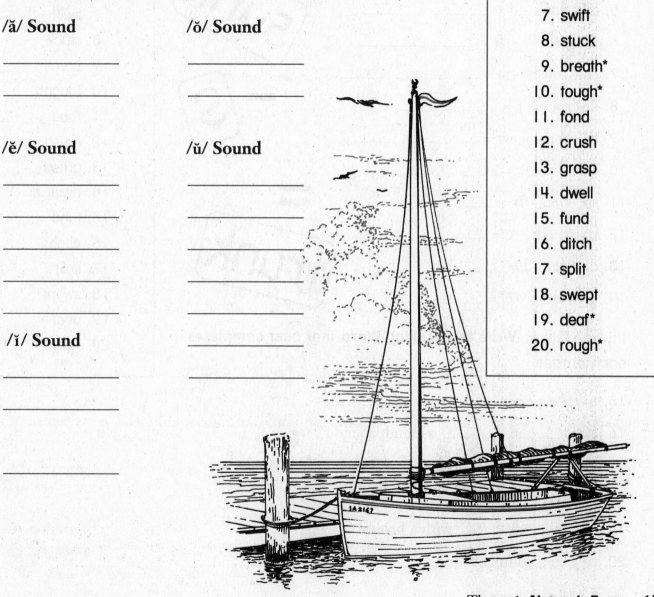

Name _____

Spelling Spree

Letter Math Add and subtract letters from the words below
to make Spelling Words. Write the new words.

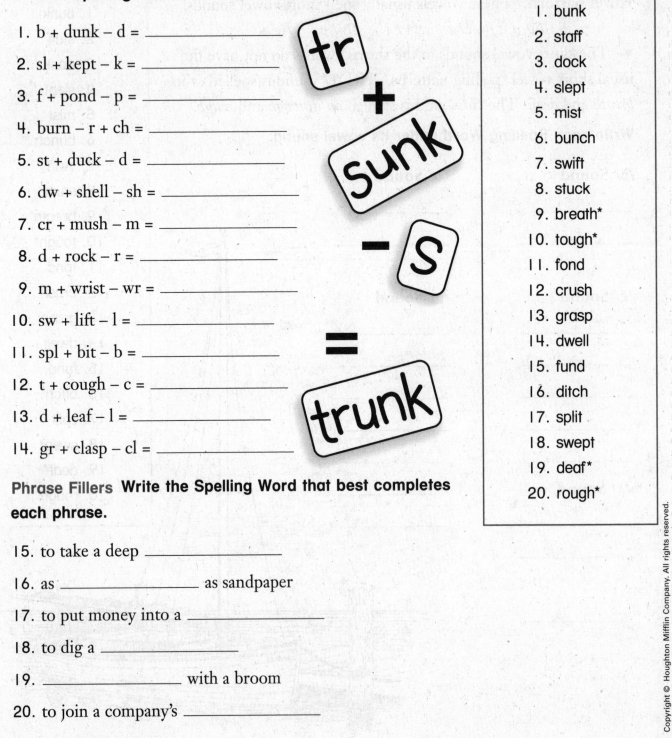

1. b + dunk – d = _____

2. sl + kept – k = _____

3. f + pond – p = _____

4. burn – r + ch = _____

5. st + duck – d = _____

6. dw + shell – sh = _____

7. cr + mush – m = _____

8. d + rock – r = _____

9. m + wrist – wr = _____

10. sw + lift – l = _____

11. spl + bit – b = _____

12. t + cough – c = _____

13. d + leaf – l = _____

14. gr + clasp – cl = _____

Spelling Words

1. bunk
2. staff
3. dock
4. slept
5. mist
6. bunch
7. swift
8. stuck
9. breath*
10. tough*
11. fond
12. crush
13. grasp
14. dwell
15. fund
16. ditch
17. split
18. swept
19. deaf*
20. rough*

Phrase Fillers Write the Spelling Word that best completes
each phrase.

15. to take a deep _____

16. as _____ as sandpaper

17. to put money into a _____

18. to dig a _____

19. _____ with a broom

20. to join a company's _____

Name _____

Proofreading and Writing

Proofreading Circle the five misspelled Spelling Words in this newspaper article. Then write each word correctly.

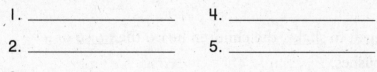

MAGPIE ISLAND — An earthquake struck yesterday, and children are reported to be stranded in the island campground. No one on the campground's staf was there at the time. An early report said that "a bunch of kids" were stouk on the island. However, it turns out that only two children are there. Rescuers in a boat are reported to be nearing the island's dok. A heavy missed has slowed the rescue effort. One rescuer said, "It's been touph going so far, but we'll get them off the island safely."

1. _____   4. _____

2. _____   5. _____

3. _____

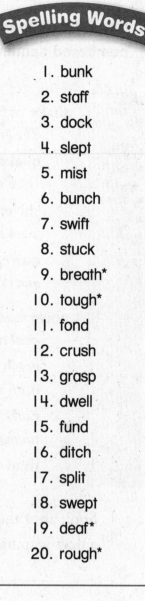

Spelling Words

1. bunk
2. staff
3. dock
4. slept
5. mist
6. bunch
7. swift
8. stuck
9. breath*
10. tough*
11. fond
12. crush
13. grasp
14. dwell
15. fund
16. ditch
17. split
18. swept
19. deaf*
20. rough*

Write a Description If you were to go to the scene of an earthquake right after it happened, what do you think you would find? What would you see? Whom would you meet?

On a separate piece of paper, write a description of the scene you might encounter. Use Spelling Words from the list.

Name _____

Synonym Shakeup

Read the definition of each thesaurus word and its synonyms. Then rewrite the numbered sentences using a different synonym for each underlined word.

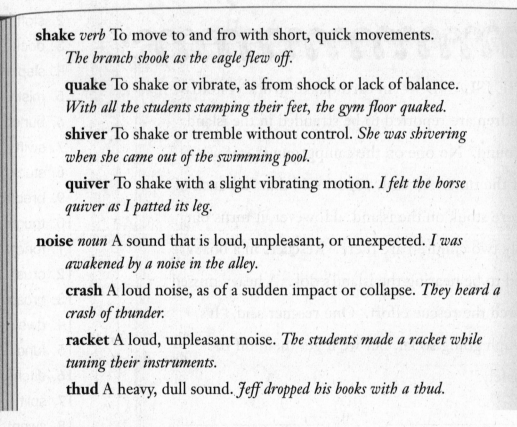

shake *verb* To move to and fro with short, quick movements. *The branch shook as the eagle flew off.*

> **quake** To shake or vibrate, as from shock or lack of balance. *With all the students stamping their feet, the gym floor quaked.*

> **shiver** To shake or tremble without control. *She was shivering when she came out of the swimming pool.*

> **quiver** To shake with a slight vibrating motion. *I felt the horse quiver as I patted its leg.*

noise *noun* A sound that is loud, unpleasant, or unexpected. *I was awakened by a noise in the alley.*

> **crash** A loud noise, as of a sudden impact or collapse. *They heard a crash of thunder.*

> **racket** A loud, unpleasant noise. *The students made a racket while tuning their instruments.*

> **thud** A heavy, dull sound. *Jeff dropped his books with a thud.*

1. Soon after the ground began to <u>shake</u>, the children heard the <u>noise</u> of a deer leaping from the bushes.

   _____

   _____

2. Jonathan began to <u>shake</u> from cold and fear, listening to the <u>noise</u> of the crows.

   _____

   _____

3. Abby's lip began to <u>shake</u> as she heard the <u>noise</u> of running footsteps.

   _____

Name _____

Sensing Danger

Kinds of Sentences There are four kinds of sentences:

1. A declarative sentence tells something and ends with a period.
   Earthquakes occur along fault lines in the earth.

2. An interrogative sentence asks a question and ends with a
   question mark.
   Can earthquakes be predicted?

3. An imperative sentence gives a request or an order and usually
   ends with a period.
   Protect your head in an earthquake.

4. An exclamatory sentence expresses strong feeling and ends
   with an exclamation mark.
   How frightening an earthquake is!

Add the correct punctuation mark to each sentence below.
Then write what kind of sentence each one is.

1. Why is the dog barking_____

   _____

2. Put him on his leash_____

   _____

3. Some animals can sense a coming earthquake_____

   _____

4. How frightened I am_____

   _____

5. The earth has stopped shaking at last_____

   _____

Name _____

On Vacation

Subjects and Predicates Every sentence has a subject. It tells whom or what the sentence is about. The complete subject includes all the words in the subject, and the simple subject is the main word or words in the complete subject.

Every sentence has a predicate too. It tells what the subject is or does. The complete predicate includes all the words in the predicate, and the simple predicate is the main word or words in the complete predicate.

Draw a slash mark (/) between the complete subject and the complete predicate in the sentences below. Then circle the simple subject and underline the simple predicate.

1. The whole family travels in our new camper.

2. Everybody helps to pitch the tent under a tree.

3. They will use a compass on their hike.

4. A good fire is difficult to build.

5. The smell of cooking is delicious to the hungry campers.

Name _____

Sentence Combining

A **compound subject** is made up of two or more simple subjects that have the same predicate. Use a connecting word such as *and* or *or* to join the simple subjects.

Jonathan yelled. **Abby** yelled.   **Jonathan and Abby** yelled.

Combine two simple subjects into one compound subject, as shown above, to make your writing clearer and less choppy.

A **compound predicate** is made up of two or more simple predicates that have the same subject. Use a connecting word such as *and* or *or* to join the simple predicates.

Moose **barked**. Moose **howled**.   Moose **barked and howled**.

Combine simple predicates into compound predicates, as shown above, to make your writing smoother.

Suppose Jonathan wrote a draft of a letter to his aunt about his vacation. Revise his letter by combining sentences. Each new sentence will have either a compound subject or a compound predicate. Only Jonathan's first sentence will remain the same.

What an exciting vacation we had! Mom broke her ankle. Mom had to go to the hospital. Abby stayed on the island. I stayed on the island during an earthquake. Moose barked. Moose warned us. The ground shook. The ground rolled. Have you ever been in an earthquake? Has Uncle Adam ever been in an earthquake?

_____

_____

_____

_____

Name _____

Writing a News Article

Jonathan and Abby Palmer experience firsthand an unforgettable event — the terror of an earthquake. Imagine you are a reporter for the *Daily Gazette*. Use the chart below to gather details for a news article about an interesting or unusual event at your school, in your neighborhood, or in your town. Answer these questions: What happened? Who was involved? When, where, and why did this event occur? How did it happen?

Who?	
What?	
When?	
Where?	
Why?	
How?	

Now use the details you gathered to write your news article on a separate sheet of paper. Include a headline and a beginning that will capture your reader's attention. Present facts in order of importance, from most to least important. Try to use quotations from eyewitnesses to bring this news event to life.

Name _____

Adding Details

A good reporter uses details to explain what happened
and to bring an event to life. Read the following news
article that might have been written about the earthquake.
Then rewrite it on the lines below, adding details from the
list to improve the article.

Details

twelve-year-old

in the woods

giant redwood

one-hundred-year-old

for several weeks

under a fallen redwood

afternoon

to the mainland

on Magpie Island

his six-year-old sister

Quake Rocks Campground

A powerful earthquake rocked an isolated
campground in California yesterday. No serious injuries
were reported. Some trees were uprooted, and a bridge
was destroyed. Two members of the Palmer family,
Jonathan and his sister Abby, were trapped during the
quake.

"I was very scared," said Jonathan Palmer. "I'm just
glad no one got hurt. My sister only had a minor cut."

The campground will be closed to visitors until the
debris is cleared and the bridge is repaired.

_____

_____

_____

_____

_____

_____

_____

_____

Name _____

Revising Your Description

Reread your description. Put a checkmark in the box for each sentence that describes your paper. Use this page to help you revise.

Rings the Bell

☐ The beginning tells my topic. The ending is satisfying.

☐ Sensory words and exact details create vivid pictures.

☐ My details are well organized and related to my topic.

☐ Voice is strong; you can tell how I feel about my topic.

☐ Sentences flow smoothly. There are almost no mistakes.

Getting Stronger

☐ The beginning and ending may be somewhat weak.

☐ More exact words and sensory details are needed.

☐ My details could be easier to follow. A few are unrelated.

☐ My voice doesn't come through clearly.

☐ Some sentences are awkward. There are a few mistakes.

Try Harder

☐ The beginning and ending are missing.

☐ There are no details. My word choices are confusing.

☐ The order is unclear. Many details are unrelated.

☐ My writing sounds flat. You can't tell how I feel.

☐ Most sentences are choppy. There are lots of mistakes.

Name _____

Writing Complete Sentences

Make each incomplete sentence complete. Change words or add extra words if you need to.

1. Being a photographer

   _____

2. Photographing nature

   _____

3. Lightning flashing in the sky

   _____

4. Chasing storms

   _____

5. Tornadoes in the distance

   _____

6. The black funnel is impressive, even far away.

   _____

7. Planes in storms

   _____

8. A bumpy ride

   _____

9. Dangerous to be out in some storms

   _____

10. Don't stand under a tree when there's lightning.

   _____

Spelling Words

Words Often Misspelled Look for familiar spelling patterns to help you remember how to spell the Spelling Words on this page. Think carefully about the parts that you find hard to spell in each word.

Write the missing letters and apostrophes in the Spelling Words below.

Spelling Words

1. enough
2. caught
3. brought
4. thought
5. every
6. ninety
7. their
8. they're
9. there
10. there's
11. know
12. knew
13. o'clock
14. we're
15. people

1. en ____ ____ ____ ____
2. c ____ ____ ____ t
3. br ____ ____ ____ ____ t
4. th ____ ____ ____ ____ t
5. ev ____ ry
6. nin ____ ty
7. th ____ ____ r
8. th ____ ____ re
9. th ____ r ____
10. th ____ ____ ____ ____ s
11. ____ ____ ow
12. ____ ____ ew
13. ____ ____ ____ lock
14. w ____ ____ ____ e
15. p ____ ____ ple

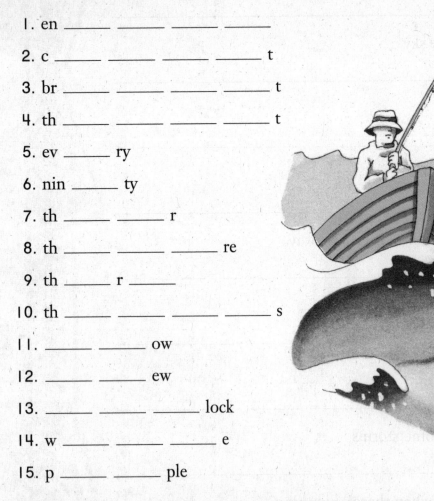

Study List On a separate piece of paper, write each Spelling Word. Check your spelling against the words on the list.

Name _____

Spelling Spree

Word Clues Write the Spelling Word that best fits each clue.

1. the sum of eighty-nine and one
2. a contraction for describing what other people are doing
3. to be aware of a fact
4. a time-telling word
5. as much as is needed
6. a word for other people's belongings
7. took along
8. a contraction for "there is"

1. _____
2. _____
3. _____
4. _____

5. _____
6. _____
7. _____
8. _____

Spelling Words

1. enough
2. caught
3. brought
4. thought
5. every
6. ninety
7. their
8. they're
9. there
10. there's
11. know
12. knew
13. o'clock
14. we're
15. people

Word Addition Write a Spelling Word by adding the beginning of the first word to the end of the second word.

then

fair

their

9. caution + fight
10. we'll + more
11. knight + flew
12. peony + steeple
13. even + wary
14. them + cure
15. think + bought

9. _____
10. _____
11. _____
12. _____
13. _____
14. _____
15. _____

Proofreading and Writing

Proofreading Circle the five misspelled Spelling Words in this announcement. Then write each word correctly.

The staff of the Science Museum is pleased to announce that our new Natural Disasters Hall will open to the public next Monday at nine oclock in the morning. We've put a lot of thaught into this exhibit, and we're sure that you'll enjoy it. Just about evry form of nature's fury is represented, from lightning to earthquakes to volcanoes. Even if you already kno a lot about the topic, we think you'll learn something new. We hope to see you their.

1. enough
2. caught
3. brought
4. thought
5. every
6. ninety
7. their
8. they're
9. there
10. there's
11. know
12. knew
13. o'clock
14. we're
15. people

1. _____ 4. _____

2. _____ 5. _____

3. _____

Write Song Titles Pick five Spelling Words from the list. Then, for each one, make up a song title that includes the word and mentions some form of Nature's Fury.

Name _____

Stormy Weather

Use words from the box to complete the diary entry below.

Vocabulary

sizzling

collide

funnel clouds

tornadoes

lightning

rotate

jagged

prairie

severe

May 10, 2000

Dear Diary,

     Today was by far the scariest day of my trip. Everything was fine as I crossed the border into Oklahoma. The highway stretched out over a _____ that seemed to go on forever. As I looked into my rear-view mirror, I spotted some dense clouds forming behind me. "I hope they aren't _____," I thought. Then I spotted a flash of _____. The clouds started to _____, slowly at first, and then faster and faster. A couple of _____ were forming right before my eyes! I realized that a _____ storm had formed behind me, and it was moving fast in my direction. The _____ bolts of lightning were getting closer. One of the tornadoes lifted a tractor into the air, spun it around, and dropped it. I watched it _____ with a shed on the ground. Lightning struck a dry bush behind me. It turned into a _____ ball of flames.

Write a sentence to end the diary entry.

_____

_____

Name _____

Selection Map

Fill in this selection map.

Pages 59–68

Page 59   Storm Chasing _____

Page 60   Warren Faidley: Storm Chaser _____

_____

Page 64   What Happens to Warren's Photos After He Takes Them?

_____

_____

Page 65   Storm Seasons and Chasing _____

_____

Page 67   Chasing Tornadoes _____

_____

Pages 69–75

One Day in the Life of a Storm Chaser

Morning _____

_____

Afternoon _____

Evening _____

_____

Name _____

An Interview with Warren Faidley

The questions below can be used to interview Warren Faidley about his life and work. Write the answer Warren might give to each question.

What is your occupation?

_____

_____

When did you first become interested in storms? Describe one of your early experiences with storms. _____

_____

What led you to become a professional storm chaser? _____

_____

_____

_____

_____

How important is it for someone in your line of work to have a good knowledge of weather patterns? Why? _____

_____

_____

What advice would you give a young person who wants to become a storm chaser? _____

Name _____

Text Tracking

Read the article below. Then complete the activity on page 35.

Hurricane Basics

A hurricane is a powerful storm with swirling winds. Hurricanes form over water in tropical parts of the North Atlantic and North Pacific Oceans. Most hurricanes in these regions occur between June and November.

Rise of a Hurricane

A hurricane does not form all at once. First, areas of low pressure develop in ocean winds. These areas, called easterly waves, then grow into a tropical depression, where winds blow at up to 31 miles per hour. As the winds pick up speed, they become a tropical storm. Finally, when the winds reach 74 miles per hour or more, and the storm is 200 to 300 miles wide, it is considered a hurricane.

Path of Destruction

The great speed of a hurricane's winds can cause severe damage. A hurricane can destroy buildings and other property when it reaches land. The force of these winds can also create huge waves. The waves along with the heavy rains may cause flooding in rivers and low-lying coastal lands. Many hurricane deaths are the result of flooding. Because of the devastating power of hurricanes, meteorologists keep a close watch on the Pacific and Atlantic Oceans during hurricane season.

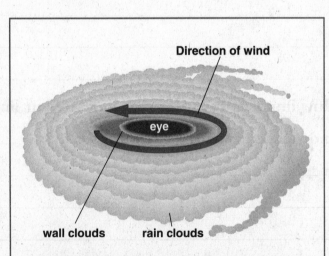

Direction of wind

eye

wall clouds   rain clouds

The winds of a hurricane rotate around the eye, which is an area of calm in the storm's center. Wall clouds surround the eye.

Text Tracking **continued**

Write words from the box to indicate the order in which these parts appear in the article on page 34. Then answer the questions.

> caption   graphic aid   headings   introduction

1. _____

2. _____

3. _____

4. _____

5. What is each paragraph about?

Paragraph 1: _____

Paragraph 2: _____

Paragraph 3: _____

6. Is the information in paragraph 2 organized by main idea and details, or by

sequence of events? _____

7. How is the information in paragraph 3 organized? _____

_____

Name _____

Stormy Syllables

**Write the underlined word using slash marks (/) between its syllables.
Then write a new sentence that uses the underlined word.**

1. The photographer changed her <u>position</u> to get a better shot of the storm.

   _____

2. A good photographer tries to <u>capture</u> the excitement of the moment.

   _____

3. Warren showed exciting <u>videos</u> of tornadoes. _____

   _____

4. I <u>wonder</u> how she was able to get so close to the lightning bolt.

   _____

5. By <u>rotating</u> his body, he could follow the circular path of the tornado.

   _____

Name _____

The /ā/, /ē/, and /ī/ Sounds

Spelling Words

1. speech
2. claim
3. strike
4. stray
5. fade
6. sign
7. leaf
8. thigh
9. thief*
10. height*
11. mild
12. waist
13. sway
14. beast
15. stain
16. fleet
17. stride
18. praise
19. slight
20. niece*

When you hear the /ā/ sound, think of the patterns
a-consonant-*e*, *ai*, and *ay*. When you hear the /ē/ sound, think of
the patterns *ea* and *ee*. When you hear the /ī/ sound, think of the
patterns i-consonant-*e*, *igh*, and *i*.

/ā/	**fade** cl**ai**m str**ay**
/ē/	l**ea**f sp**ee**ch
/ī/	str**i**ke th**igh** s**i**gn

▶ The long vowel sounds in the starred words have different
spelling patterns. The /ē/ sound in *thief* and in *niece* is spelled *ie*.
The /ī/ sound in *height* is spelled *eigh*.

Write each Spelling Word under its vowel sound.

/ā/	/ē/	/ī/
_____	_____	_____
_____	_____	_____
_____	_____	_____
_____	_____	_____
_____	_____	_____
_____	_____	_____

Name _____

Spelling Spree

Find a Rhyme For each sentence write a Spelling Word that rhymes with the underlined word and makes sense in the sentence.

1. On what <u>day</u> did you last see the _____ cat?

2. It looks like the _____ got washed out by the <u>rain</u>.

3. She liked to _____ down the beach at low <u>tide</u>.

4. They swam out to <u>meet</u> the _____ of ships.

5. How <u>high</u> on the _____ did the ball hit you?

6. His _____ asked for another <u>piece</u> of pie.

7. The police <u>chief</u> took credit for catching the _____.

8. The young <u>child</u> liked _____ food better than spicy food.

Crack the Code Some Spelling Words have been written in the code below. Use the code to figure out each word. Then write the word correctly.

CODE:	R	V	L	O	C	A	D	X	P	T	Y	Q	J	N	E	I	M
LETTER:	a	b	c	e	f	g	h	i	l	m	n	p	r	s	t	w	y

9. LPRXT _____

10. IRXNE _____

11. VORNE _____   15. NPXADE _____

12. NQOOLD _____   16. NIRM _____

13. NXAY _____   17. QJRXNO _____

14. DOXADE _____   18. PORC _____

Spelling Words

1. speech
2. claim
3. strike
4. stray
5. fade
6. sign
7. leaf
8. thigh
9. thief*
10. height*
11. mild
12. waist
13. sway
14. beast
15. stain
16. fleet
17. stride
18. praise
19. slight
20. niece*

Proofreading and Writing

Proofreading Circle the five misspelled Spelling Words in this
weather log entry. Then write each word correctly.

May 20 — There was a report today of a lightning streik at
the shopping mall outside town. The same storm passed
over our house, with heavy winds. It made the trees sweigh
so much that I was sure at least one would fall. The winds
started to faide before that happened, though. On the news,
the reporter said that the base of the storm clouds was
actually at a hight of over 5,000 feet. The weather
tomorrow is supposed to be mild, with a slite chance
of rain.

1. _____

2. _____

3. _____

4. _____

5. _____

1. speech
2. claim
3. strike
4. stray
5. fade
6. sign
7. leaf
8. thigh
9. thief*
10. height*
11. mild
12. waist
13. sway
14. beast
15. stain
16. fleet
17. stride
18. praise
19. slight
20. niece*

Write a Storm Warning Storm chasers are able to provide
firsthand, "you are there" reports of storms because they chase the
storms.

**On a separate sheet of paper, write the script of a storm
warning that a storm chaser might issue by radio. Use Spelling
Words from the list.**

Name _____

Words in Their Places

Read each set of words, and decide which two could be the guide words and which one the entry word on a dictionary page. Then in the columns below, write the guide words under the correct heading, and the entry word beside them.

trout	weather	prance	durable	chase
trust	wayward	practice	dust	charter
tropical	weave	prairie	dusky	chatterbox

Guide Words		Entry Word
_____	_____	_____
_____	_____	_____
_____	_____	_____
_____	_____	_____
_____	_____	_____

Name _____

It's a Twister!

Conjunctions The words *and, or,* and *but* are **conjunctions**. A conjunction may be used to join words in a sentence or to join sentences. Use *and* to add information. Use *or* to give a choice. Use *but* to show contrast.

■ Clouds **and** wind signal a coming storm.
   This conjunction joins words.
■ I saw lightning, **and** I heard thunder.
   This conjunction joins sentences.

Write the conjunction *and, or,* or *but* to best complete each sentence. Then decide whether each conjunction you wrote joins words or joins sentences. Write W after a sentence in which words are joined. Write S after a sentence in which sentences are joined.

1. Kansas _____ Oklahoma have many tornadoes. ____

2. Warren Faidley chases tornadoes _____ thunderstorms. ____

3. Warren has special equipment, _____ he has a special vehicle to carry it. ____

4. I have never seen a tornado, _____ I have seen lightning many times. ____

5. Go into a cellar _____ another low place if you see a funnel cloud. ____

Name _____

In Focus

Compound Sentences A **compound sentence** is made by joining two closely related simple sentences with a comma and a conjunction.

I like to read.
You like to write. } I like to read, but you like to write.

Draw a line from each simple sentence in column A to the most closely related sentence in column B. Read all the choices before you decide.

A	**B**
1. Zoe takes photos for the school paper	Zoe took pictures of the musicians.
2. Should Zoe use color film	Tom writes stories for the paper.
3. Color photos are nice	the photos in our newspaper are black and white.
4. Tom wrote about the school concert	should she use black and white film?

Now, write the sentences above and join them by using conjunctions instead of lines. Don't forget to put a comma before each conjunction!

1. _____

_____

2. _____

_____

3. _____

_____

4. _____

_____

Name _____

Lightning Strikes!

Correcting Run-on Sentences A **run-on sentence** occurs when a writer runs one simple sentence into another without using a comma and a conjunction between them. The sentence below is a run-on sentence.

> Marco lives on a farm his cousin likes to visit him there.

Correct run-on sentences in your writing by inserting a comma and conjunction to make a compound sentence:

> Marco lives on a farm ^, and^ his cousin likes to visit him there.

Marco is excited and has quickly typed an e-mail message to his cousin Jamie. Revise Marco's message by adding missing commas and conjunctions.

> Lightning struck near our farm I saw
> it happen. The bolt hit an old tree on
> top of a hill, the tree split in half.
> There was a loud boom the air
> crackled. It was scary I was safe in
> our house at the bottom of the hill.
> Should I send you a picture of the
> tree do you want to visit to see it for
> yourself?

Name _____

Responding to a Prompt

A **prompt** is a direction that asks for a written answer of one or more paragraphs. Read the following prompts.

Prompt 1

What job do you think is the most difficult or dangerous? Explain why you think it is difficult or dangerous.

Prompt 2

Think about how Warren Faidley customized Shadow Chaser for chasing tornadoes. Describe how you would customize a vehicle for a specific task.

Choose one prompt and use the chart below to help you write a response. First, list key words in the prompt. Then jot down main ideas and details you might include. Finally, number your main ideas, beginning with *1*, from most to least important.

Key Words	Main Ideas	Details

Write your response on a separate sheet of paper. Start by restating the prompt. Then write your main ideas and supporting details in order of importance from most to least important, or from least to most important.

Name _____

Capitalizing and Punctuating Sentences

A fifth-grade class was given this writing prompt: **Warren Faidley is a storm chaser. Summarize what he does for a living.** One fifth grader wrote the response below but forgot to check for capitalization and punctuation errors.

Use these proofreading marks to add the necessary capital letters and end punctuation.

⊙ Add a period.
≡ Make a capital letter.
∧! Add an exclamation point.
∧? Add a question mark.

what does Warren Faidley do for a living He follows dangerous storms
for example, he tracks down tornadoes and hurricanes then he
photographs lightning striking the earth and funnel clouds whirling in
the sky. if he has been successful, he can sell his dramatic photos to
magazines, newspapers, and other publications What a risky but
exciting job storm chasers have

Name _____

Volcanic Activity

Write each word from the box under the correct category below.

Description of Hot Lava

_____

Earth Layer

_____

Materials in a Volcano

_____

_____

_____

Volcano Parts

_____

_____

Event

_____

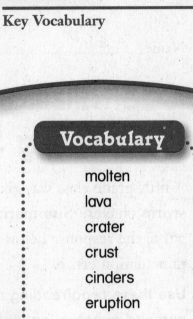

Vocabulary

molten
lava
crater
crust
cinders
eruption
magma
summit

Now choose at least four words from the box. Use them to write a short paragraph describing an exploding volcano.

_____

_____

_____

_____

_____

Name _____

Category Chart

Fill in the boxes in each category.

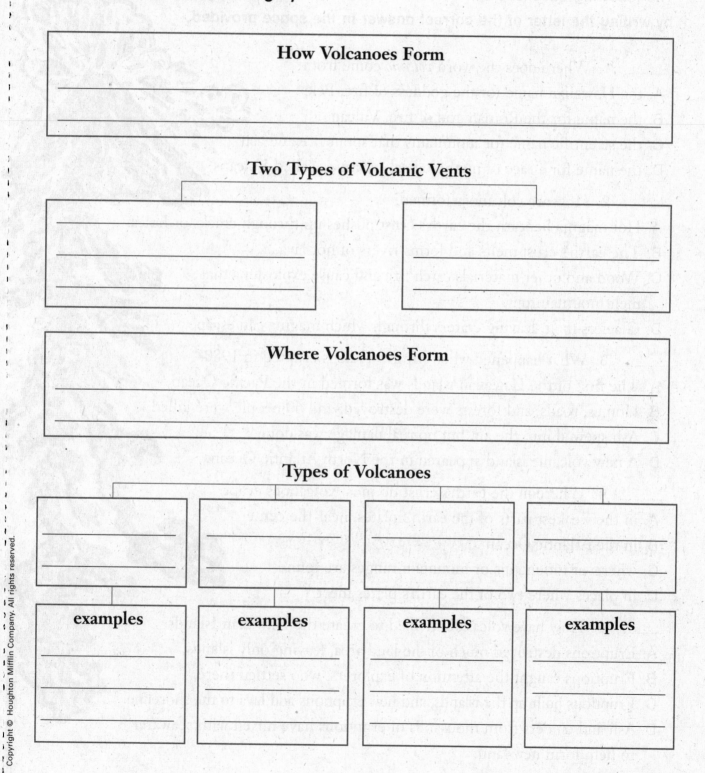

How Volcanoes Form

_____

_____

Two Types of Volcanic Vents

Where Volcanoes Form

_____

_____

Types of Volcanoes

examples   **examples**   **examples**   **examples**

Name _____

Show What You Know!

The following questions ask about volcanoes. Answer each question by writing the letter of the correct answer in the space provided.

_____ 1. Where does the word *volcano* come from?

A. the Hawaiian name for the goddess of fire, Pele

B. the name for the Roman god of fire, Vulcan

C. the scientific name for mountains that spout fire and ash

D. the name for a race of mythological creatures called Vulcans

_____ 2. How are volcanoes formed?

A. Hot magma beneath the earth's crust pushes up through cracks or holes.

B. The earth's crust melts and forms rivers of hot lava.

C. Wood and other materials catch fire and cause explosions that melt mountaintops.

D. Glaciers melt, leaving craters through which magma can escape.

_____ 3. What happened when Mt. St. Helens erupted in 1980?

A. The first of the Hawaiian islands was formed in the Pacific Ocean.

B. Homes, roads, and forests were destroyed, and 60 people were killed.

C. Ash spewed into the air, but no real damage was done.

D. A new volcanic island appeared in the North Atlantic Ocean.

_____ 4. Where in the earth's crust do most volcanoes erupt?

A. in the weakest parts of the earth's plates, near the center

B. in the Atlantic Ocean

C. wherever mountains or mountain ranges are found

D. in places where two of the earth's plates meet

_____ 5. How have volcanoes helped to create the Hawaiian Islands?

A. Eruptions destroyed much of the land area, leaving only islands.

B. Eruptions caught the attention of explorers, who settled there.

C. Eruptions built up the islands, and new eruptions add lava to the shoreline.

D. Ash and cinders from thousands of eruptions have mixed with seawater to help form new land.

Name _____

Classifying Clouds

Read the article. Then complete the activity on page 50.

Clouds

Clouds come in a variety of forms and colors. They occur at different heights. Some are made of water and some of ice. With all these differences, a good way to identify clouds is by their groups.

Clouds are grouped by how high above the earth they are found. Low clouds are usually not more than 6,000 feet above sea level. They include stratus and stratocumulus clouds. A stratus cloud looks like a smooth sheet, while stratocumulus clouds are lumpy. They look like fluffy gray piles of cotton.

Middle clouds form between 6,000 and 20,000 feet. They include altostratus, altocumulus, and nimbostratus clouds. An altostratus cloud forms a white or gray sheet. Altocumulus clouds appear as fluffy piles that may be separated or connected in a lumpy mass. Nimbostratus clouds look like a smooth, gray layer. Rain or snow often falls from them, making them hard to see.

High clouds form above 20,000 feet. Unlike other kinds of clouds, which are made of water droplets, these clouds consist of ice crystals. Cirrus, cirrostratus, and cirrocumulus are types of high clouds. Cirrus clouds are very high in the sky and have a feathery appearance. A cirrostratus cloud is a very thin cloud layer. Cirrocumulus clouds look like millions of bits of fluff high in the sky.

Name _____

Classifying Clouds continued

Follow the directions or answer the questions based on the article.

1. Add the names of any cloud types mentioned in the
   article that are missing from this chart.

low	middle	high
stratus	altostratus	cirrus

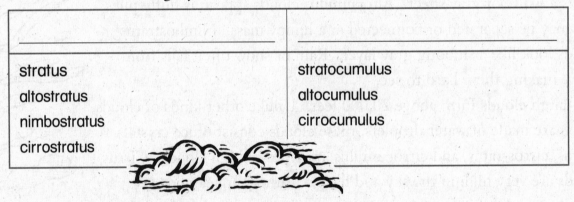

2. How are the clouds in this chart classified? _____
   Write the correct category for each list of clouds in this chart.

_____	_____
stratus	stratocumulus
altostratus	altocumulus
nimbostratus	cirrocumulus
cirrostratus	

3. How are the clouds in this chart classified? _____
   Add the names of cloud types not listed to the correct column.

water	ice
stratus	cirrus
altostratus	cirrostratus
nimbostratus	

Name _____

Construct a Word

Read each sentence. Then, using two or three columns in the chart, build a word containing the root *-struct* or *-rupt* that completes the sentence. Write the word on the line.

de	rupt	ive
dis	struct	or
con		ion
e		ure
inter		
in		

1. Sam's swimming _____
   taught him how to do the backstroke.

2. I watched the _____ of the
   volcano from my window.

3. We helped our cousin _____ a tree house
   in the backyard.

4. The hurricane left a path of _____
   along the coast.

5. Please don't _____ me when
   I'm talking!

6. The noise in the hall was very _____
   during our rehearsal.

7. The leak was caused by a _____
   in the pipeline.

8. The children sat on top of the climbing
   _____ in the playground.

Name _____

The /ō/, /o͞o/, and /yo͞o/ Sounds

When you hear the /ō/ sound, think of the patterns *o*-consonant-*e*, *oa*, *ow*, and *o*. When you hear the /o͞o/ and the /yo͞o/ sounds, think of the patterns *u*-consonant-*e*, *ue*, *ew*, *oo*, *ui*, and *ou*.

/ō/   sl**o**pe, b**oa**st, thr**ow**n, str**o**ll

/o͞o/ or /yo͞o/   r**u**le, cl**ue**, d**ew**, ch**oo**se, cr**ui**se, r**ou**te

Write each Spelling Word under its vowel sound.

/ō/ Sound

_____   _____

_____   _____

_____   _____

/o͞o/ or /yo͞o/ Sounds

_____   _____

_____   _____

_____   _____

_____   _____

_____

Spelling Words

1. thrown
2. stole
3. clue
4. dew
5. choose
6. rule
7. boast
8. cruise
9. stroll
10. route
11. mood
12. loaf
13. growth
14. youth
15. slope
16. bruise
17. loose
18. rude
19. flow
20. flute

Name _____

Spelling Spree

Letter Swap **Write a Spelling Word by changing the underlined letter to a different letter.**

1. st<u>a</u>le _____
2. lo<u>us</u>e _____
3. clu<u>b</u> _____
4. loa<u>d</u> _____
5. r<u>o</u>le _____
6. <u>t</u>oast _____
7. moo<u>n</u> _____
8. de<u>n</u> _____

Word Switch **Write a Spelling Word to replace each underlined definition in the sentences. Write your words on the lines.**

9. My parents are taking a <u>sea voyage for pleasure</u> on that ship.
10. Which item did you <u>pick out</u> from the catalog?
11. Many people are active in sports in their <u>time of life before adulthood.</u>
12. You can use a ruler to measure the <u>increase in size</u> of the plant.
13. I play the <u>woodwind instrument shaped like a tube</u> in the band.
14. A clerk should never be <u>lacking in courtesy</u> to a shopper.
15. Would you care to <u>walk slowly</u> down the beach with me?

9. _____ 13. _____
10. _____ 14. _____
11. _____ 15. _____
12. _____

Spelling Words

1. thrown
2. stole
3. clue
4. dew
5. choose
6. rule
7. boast
8. cruise
9. stroll
10. route
11. mood
12. loaf
13. growth
14. youth
15. slope
16. bruise
17. loose
18. rude
19. flow
20. flute

_f_ _blow_

Theme 1: **Nature's Fury** 53

Name _____

Proofreading and Writing

Proofreading Circle the five misspelled Spelling Words in this paragraph from a personal narrative. Then write each word correctly.

Our roote led us up the side of the volcano. We had just reached an old area of lava flo when we heard a rumbling noise from above. Hikers ahead of us on the trail had knocked some rocks loose! The avalanche was heading down the sloap of the mountain, straight for us. In the rush to reach safety, I tripped and was thron off the trail. Luckily, the mass of rocks passed me by, and all I got was a briuse on my leg.

1. _____
2. _____
3. _____
4. _____
5. _____

Spelling Words

1. thrown
2. stole
3. clue
4. dew
5. choose
6. rule
7. boast
8. cruise
9. stroll
10. route
11. mood
12. loaf
13. growth
14. youth
15. slope
16. bruise
17. loose
18. rude
19. flow
20. flute

Write a List of Safety Tips What safety tips would it be good to keep in mind when exploring a volcano?

On a separate sheet of paper, list some tips for volcano explorers. Use Spelling Words from the list.

Name _____

Missing Definitions

The dictionary entries below include an entry word and a sample sentence, but they are missing the definition. Read each sample sentence and use it to help you fill in the definition.

1. ancient (**ān′** shənt) _____

   The dinosaur tracks in the rocks show how ancient they are.

2. astonishing (ə **stŏn′** ĭ shĭng) _____

   It was astonishing to see it snowing in the middle of July.

3. awaken (ə **wā′** kən) _____

   The campers awaken at the first light of dawn.

4. damage (**dăm′** ĭj) _____

   Using too much water can damage the plants.

5. extinct (ĭk **stĭngkt′**) _____

   Since its last eruption a thousand years ago, the volcano has been extinct.

6. fiery (**fīr′** ē) _____

   The flames made a fiery glow in the sky.

7. spout (spout) _____

   Water from the fountain spouts into the air.

8. summit (**sŭm′** ĭt) _____

   After a long hard climb, we reached the summit of the mountain.

Name _____

Finding Your Way

Singular and Plural Nouns A **singular noun** names one person, one place, one thing, or one idea. A **plural noun** names more than one person, place, thing, or idea. To decide how to form a plural, look at the end of the singular noun. Here are four rules to study:

1. To most singular nouns, add *-s* to form the plural.
2. If a singular noun ends in *s*, *ss*, *x*, *ch*, or *sh*, add *-es* to form the plural.
3. For singular nouns ending with a vowel plus *y*, add *-s* to form the plural.
4. If a singular noun ends in a consonant plus *y*, change the *y* to *i* and add *-es*.

bench
table
tree
fox
fireplace
tent
daisy
bush
bus
pathway

Conrad and Carmen have drawn a map of a campground they are visiting. Label each landmark on the map with a plural noun. Use nouns from the list.

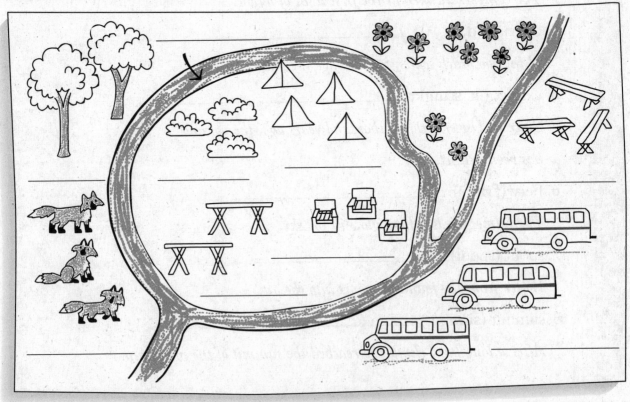

Grammar Skill More
Plural Nouns

Name _____

Science Fair

More Plural Nouns Here are a few more rules for forming plurals:

1. To form the plural of some nouns ending in *f* or *fe*, change the *f* to *v* and add -*es*. For others ending in *f*, simply add -*s*.

2. To form the plural of nouns ending with a vowel plus *o*, add -*s*.

3. To form the plural of nouns ending with a consonant plus *o*, add -*s* or -*es*.

4. Some nouns have special plural forms.

5. Some nouns are the same in the singular and the plural.

For the science fair, Jody made a model of the volcano Mount Saint Helens and wrote a report about it. Jody isn't sure how to form the plural of some words in her report. She made a list of these words.

Write the plural next to each word on Jody's list. Check your dictionary if you are unsure of a plural.

leaf _____

child _____

volcano _____

man _____

ash _____

home _____

deer _____

woman _____

plant _____

mouse _____

Name _____

Roaming Through the Woods

Using Exact Nouns You can make your writing more lively and interesting by replacing general nouns with more specific ones. Here is an example of writing with a general noun:

> For my birthday, I received **several things**.

A reader does not know what the person received. Here is the same sentence revised to use more specific nouns:

> For my birthday, I received **a book about sports legends, a basketball, and basketball shoes**.

Read the following paragraph. Revise the general nouns in bold type by replacing them with a more specific noun from the box.

a rabbit

dragonfly

maples and oaks

Duck Pond

minnows

peanut butter

sandwiches

my ankles

mint

bark

sneakers

Yesterday, Aunt Dorothy and I walked through the woods to the **pond**. My aunt knows much about nature. On our way, she pointed out **trees** and showed me how to recognize them by their leaves and **stuff**. She even taught me how to recognize **a plant** by its minty smell! When we arrived at the pond, I saw a **bug** hovering low over the water. Because it was a warm day, I took off my **shoes** and waded in the pond. The water was so clear I could see **things** swimming around **me**. After that, we ate our **food**. On the way home, we saw **an animal** hop across the path.

Name _____

Writing a Paragraph of Information

Read the following paragraph of information from page 87 of *Volcanoes*.

Volcanoes are formed by cracks or holes that poke through the earth's crust. Magma pushes its way up through the cracks. This is called a volcanic eruption. When magma pours onto the surface it is called lava. . . . As lava cools, it hardens to form rock.

Now get ready to write your own paragraph of information about volcanoes. Use the following graphic organizer to help you organize your paragraph.

Topic
_____

Topic Sentence
_____
_____

Supporting Sentences
_____
_____
_____
_____

Now, write your paragraph of information on a separate sheet of paper. Arrange your supporting sentences in a logical order, and make sure all of the sentences contain facts about the topic.

Name _____

Correcting Sentence Fragments

**A sentence fragment is a group of words that is missing either a
subject or a predicate. The following groups of words are sentence
fragments. Turn them into complete sentences by adding either
a subject or a predicate. Write the complete sentence
on the lines.**

1. Many of the world's active volcanoes.

_____

_____

2. Clouds of hot ash.

_____

_____

3. Buries plants and animals.

_____

_____

4. The blast of an eruption.

_____

_____

5. Are seriously injured or killed.

_____

_____

Name _____

Tornado Report

Use the words in the box to complete this news report about a tornado.

> ## Vocabulary
>
> alert   flickering   reception   bolting   lull   huddled

A Category 4 tornado touched down in central Nebraska at approximately 4:30 P.M. yesterday. A severe weather _____ was issued by the National Weather Service before the storm struck. However, many residents lost power and had no _____ on their radios or televisions at the time.

    Witnesses who still had power reported that their lights were _____ on and off as the twister approached. One man remembered _____ for the basement of his house as he heard the storm draw nearer. A local woman recalled a period of absolute stillness right before the tornado hit. During this _____, she wondered if the tornado had passed by. Most local residents _____ in the center of their basements until the storm passed, following safety guidelines published in yesterday's newspaper.

Name _____

Storm Sequences

	🌪 *Night of the Twisters*	❄ *Blizzard!*
First, a storm		
The people in the selection go		
Then,		
At the end of the selection,		

Name _____

Describing Twisters

Compare and contrast the descriptions of tornadoes in *Night of the Twisters* and *Eye of the Storm*. Use the categories on the chart to list details from each selection.

	Night of the Twisters	*Eye of the Storm*
Vivid verbs		
Sensory details		
Figurative language		

Name _____

Emergency Response Words

Write each word from the box in the space next to its meaning.

Vocabulary

immense	treacherous	desperate
ominous	stranded	floes

1. unable to reach safety _____

2. very, very dangerous _____

3. frantic and willing to try anything _____

4. chunks of floating ice _____

5. signaling danger or trouble _____

6. huge _____

Now choose four words from the box. Use them to write a short paragraph describing a winter storm you have experienced or read about.

_____

_____

_____

_____

_____

_____

Name _____

Test Practice

Use the three steps you've learned to choose the best answer for these questions about *Blizzard!* Fill in the circle for the best answer in the answer row at the bottom of the page.

1. Why did the author write about the ice floes in *Blizzard!*?

   A to compare different types of natural disasters

   B to tell a true story about a dangerous situation

   C to explain how to cross ice floes safely

   D to persuade people not to cross frozen rivers

2. Why did ladder operators raise their prices when they saw the tugboats?

   F because people would soon need to leave the ice

   G because people would want to come see the tugboats

   H because crossing on broken ice would be more exciting

   J because people would want to ride on the tugboats

3. What caused the ice to begin moving toward the sea?

   A the weight of the people   **C** the windy conditions

   B the shifting of the tide   **D** the heavy snowfall

4. **Connecting/Comparing** In what way are the people who walked onto the ice different from storm chasers such as Warren in *Eye of the Storm*?

   F The people on the ice used special equipment.

   G The people on the ice were scientists.

   H Storm chasers' work is not helpful to others.

   J Storm chasers weigh the dangers before acting.

ANSWER ROWS   1 Ⓐ Ⓑ Ⓒ Ⓓ   3 Ⓐ Ⓑ Ⓒ Ⓓ
              2 Ⓕ Ⓖ Ⓗ Ⓙ   4 Ⓕ Ⓖ Ⓗ Ⓙ

Continue on page 66.

Test Practice continued

5. Why did most people ignore the police?

   A They did not like figures of authority.

   B They did not care about safety.

   C They were eager for adventure.

   D They did not understand the police.

6. Who provided most of the first-hand information about the rescue of the floaters?

   F the author

   G a policeman

   H one of the rescued men

   J a newspaper reporter

7. Why do you think the spectators cheered after the last floaters were rescued?

   A They enjoyed the drama.

   B They were relieved everyone was safe.

   C They admired the tugboats.

   D They admired the floaters.

8. **Connecting/Comparing** In what way was the family dog in *Earthquake Terror* like the dogs in *Blizzard!*?

   F Both dogs sensed danger.

   G Both dogs protected people.

   H Both dogs barked warnings.

   J Both dogs rescued others.

ANSWER ROWS 5 (A) (B) (C) (D)   7 (A) (B) (C) (D)
6 (F) (G) (H) (J)   8 (F) (G) (H) (J)

Name _____

How Is It Organized?

Read the article. Then complete the activity below.

Tsunamis[1]

A tsunami (tsoo NAH mee)[2] is a giant ocean wave produced by an undersea earthquake, landslide, or volcanic eruption. Most tsunamis occur in the Pacific Ocean. The wave may only be a few feet high in the open ocean, but as it approaches a coastline it can rise to a height of over 100 feet. How fast a tsunami travels depends on the depth of the water it is traveling through. In deep waters, a tsunami can travel 600 miles per hour. As it nears shore, however, the wave might slow to about 100 miles per hour.

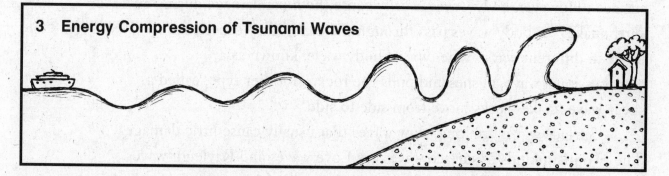

3 Energy Compression of Tsunami Waves

Use a word or phrase in the box to label each of the numbered text features in the article. Write your responses on the lines below.

1. _____

2. _____

3. _____

diagram

pronunciation key

title

Answer the questions.

4. What is the heading of the diagram?

_____

5. How is the information in the article organized?

_____

Name _____

Earth Waves

Read the article. Then complete the activity below.

Earthquakes and Seismic Waves

    An earthquake occurs when huge masses of rock shift and break below and on the surface of the earth. This movement releases energy that travels in all directions in the form of vibrations called seismic waves. These waves are classified according to how they travel. Fast vibrations known as **body waves** move through the earth. Slower **surface waves** move along the earth's surface.

    Body waves travel faster deep within the earth than near the earth's surface. However, body waves usually cause the most damage during an earthquake. As body waves pass through the earth, they cause rock to move in different ways. One type of body wave, known as a compressional wave, pushes and pulls the rock. Another type, called a shear wave, makes rocks move from side to side.

    Surface waves are long, slow waves that usually cause little damage. The two main kinds of surface waves are Love waves and Rayleigh waves. Love waves move the ground from side to side. Rayleigh waves make the surface of the earth roll like waves on the ocean.

Answer the questions.

How are seismic waves classified?

_____

Add names or categories that are missing from this chart.

Types of _____	
Body	_____
_____ shear	Love

Name _____

Decide Where to Divide

Read each sentence. Rewrite the underlined word with a slash or slashes to divide the syllables. After the word, write which of the following patterns helped you decide where to divide.

VCCV	VCV (long first vowel)
CVVC	VCV (short first vowel)

1. The sunset <u>glimmered</u> orange on the sparkling waves.

   _____

2. A <u>giant</u> wave gathered strength and smashed into the shore.

   _____

3. A <u>funnel</u> cloud threatened to reach the ground.

   _____

4. The family took <u>shelter</u> in their basement.

   _____

5. The tornado left the house with several <u>broken</u> windows.

   _____

6. The <u>reporter</u> wrote an eyewitness account of the storm.

   _____

Name _____

Meaning Match

Read the definitions and the four sentences at the bottom of the page. In the blank space after each sentence, write the correct meaning for the underlined word.

fragment (frăg´ mənt) *n.* **1.** A piece or part broken off or separated from a whole: *She picked up a fragment of the broken plate.* **2.** Something incomplete or not finished. *The note contained only a sentence fragment.* —*v.* to break into pieces. *The thin ice will fragment at the slightest pressure.*

particular (pər tĭk´ yə lər) *adj.* **1.** Of or for a single person, group, or thing. *Each group did its particular job.* **2.** Unique; having to do only with a certain person or thing. *The dog has a particular whine when it is hungry.* **3.** Demanding close attention to detail. *My aunt is very particular about housekeeping.* —*n.* a single item, fact, or detail.

vent (vĕnt) n. An opening through which liquid or gas can pass through or escape. *Hot air from the dryer flows through a hose to a vent in the wall.* —*v.* to express; give utterance to. *People vented their frustrations about the long ticket lines.*

1. Ash, rock, and fumes spewed outward through a <u>vent</u> in the side of the volcano. _____

   _____

2. The blast left a <u>particular</u> track of devastation.

   _____

3. The eruption sent <u>fragments</u> of rock flying in all directions.

   _____

4. Sam had to <u>vent</u> his anger that we were not taking the volcano threat seriously.

   _____

Name _____

Spelling Review

Write Spelling Words from the list on this page to answer the questions.

1–9. Which nine words have a short vowel sound?

1. _____   6. _____

2. _____   7. _____

3. _____   8. _____

4. _____   9. _____

5. _____

10–19. Which ten words have the /ā/, /ē/, or /ī/ sound?

10. _____   15. _____

11. _____   16. _____

12. _____   17. _____

13. _____   18. _____

14. _____   19. _____

20–30. Which eleven words have the /ō/, /yo͞o/, or /o͞o/ sound?

20. _____   26. _____

21. _____   27. _____

22. _____   28. _____

23. _____   29. _____

24. _____   30. _____

25. _____

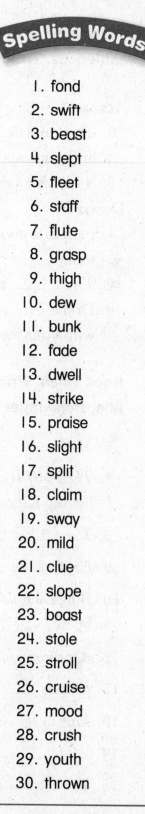

Spelling Words

1. fond
2. swift
3. beast
4. slept
5. fleet
6. staff
7. flute
8. grasp
9. thigh
10. dew
11. bunk
12. fade
13. dwell
14. strike
15. praise
16. slight
17. split
18. claim
19. sway
20. mild
21. clue
22. slope
23. boast
24. stole
25. stroll
26. cruise
27. mood
28. crush
29. youth
30. thrown

Spelling Spree

Puzzle Power Use the Spelling Words to complete the
sentences. Write the words in the puzzle.

Across

3. The animals _____
   in the forest.
5. A lion is a large _____.

Down

1. I am in a good _____
   today.
2. The _____ is very steep.
4. Don't _____ that flower
   with your foot!

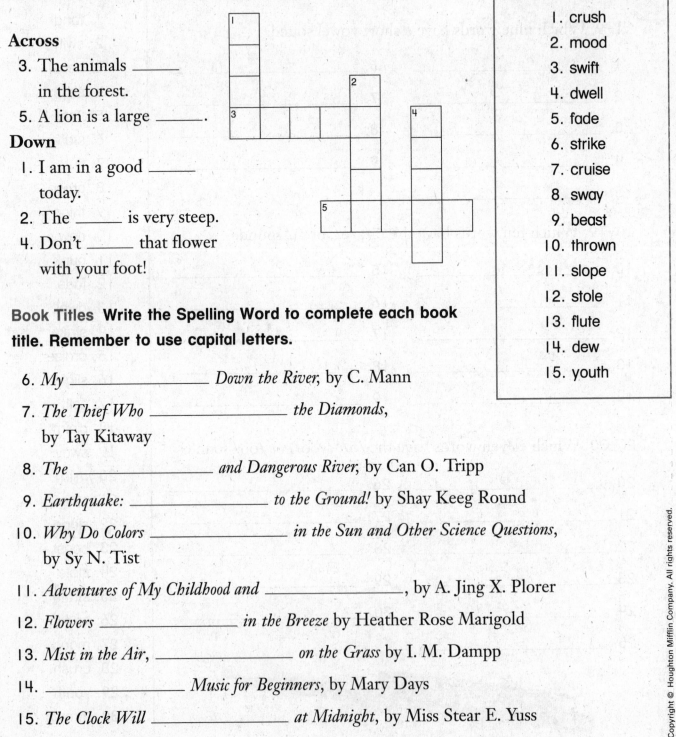

Spelling Words

1. crush
2. mood
3. swift
4. dwell
5. fade
6. strike
7. cruise
8. sway
9. beast
10. thrown
11. slope
12. stole
13. flute
14. dew
15. youth

Book Titles Write the Spelling Word to complete each book
title. Remember to use capital letters.

6. *My _____ Down the River,* by C. Mann

7. *The Thief Who _____ the Diamonds,*
   by Tay Kitaway

8. *The _____ and Dangerous River,* by Can O. Tripp

9. *Earthquake: _____ to the Ground!* by Shay Keeg Round

10. *Why Do Colors _____ in the Sun and Other Science Questions,*
    by Sy N. Tist

11. *Adventures of My Childhood and _____,* by A. Jing X. Plorer

12. *Flowers _____ in the Breeze* by Heather Rose Marigold

13. *Mist in the Air, _____ on the Grass* by I. M. Dampp

14. _____ *Music for Beginners,* by Mary Days

15. *The Clock Will _____ at Midnight,* by Miss Stear E. Yuss

Name _____

Proofreading and Writing

Proofreading Circle the six misspelled Spelling Words in this newspaper article. Then write each word correctly.

At 11:30 last night, a milde earthquake gently rocked the city. Little damage was reported, and some people sleept right through it. This morning Helen and Joe Dalton boste that they were not afraid. There was only slite damage downtown. With prayse for his workers, the mayor said, "My staf responded quickly to all questions."

1. _____   4. _____

2. _____   5. _____

3. _____   6. _____

Spelling Words

1. slept
2. praise
3. fond
4. clue
5. staff
6. thigh
7. stroll
8. slight
9. claim
10. fleet
11. mild
12. grasp
13. split
14. bunk
15. boast

In the News **A reporter takes notes after an earthquake. Complete his ideas by writing Spelling Words in the blanks.**

- No one is _____ of surprises like this.

- Scientists have no _____ about why this quake occurred at night.

- It is a strange time to _____ through town!

- I'd rather be in my _____ sleeping.

- A man has cuts on his _____ and ankle.

- A large _____ of fire trucks roars by.

- Large crevice in ground. Oak street is _____ in two!

- It's hard to fully _____ the power of a quake.

- Some people _____ that animals can predict earthquakes.

➤ **Write a Safety Plan** **On a separate sheet of paper, write about what you should do in an earthquake. Use the Spelling Review Words.**

The Twister Is Right on Top of Us!

Write what kind of sentence each is—declarative, interrogative, imperative, or exclamatory.

1. The windows are breaking! _____

2. Cover your face with a towel. _____

3. We must stay together. _____

4. Has the tornado passed? _____

Identify each sentence type. Then rewrite it as the type shown below.

5. You should help your brother. _____

   Imperative: _____

6. The rain will stop soon. _____

   Interrogative: _____

7. Does someone have a flashlight? _____

   Declarative: _____

8. The police are outside. _____

   Exclamatory: _____

Name _____

Conjunction Functions

Circle each conjunction in the sentences below. Write *compound sentence* after each compound sentence.

1. A blanket of snow covered Manhattan and Brooklyn.

   _____

2. The ice on the river looked thick, but no one walked out on it.

   _____

3. A boy put a ladder onto the ice and jumped up and down.

   _____

4. The boy held the ladder, and people climbed down to the ice.

   _____

5. People stepped carefully onto the ice, but dogs ran onto it recklessly.

   _____

6. Were there more dogs or more people on the ice?

   _____ .

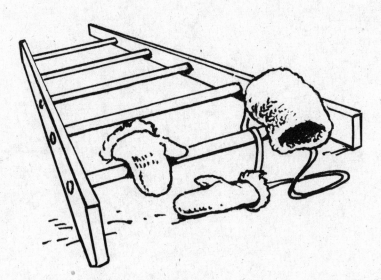

Name _____

A Reporter's Tale

Use the words in the box to complete the news reporter's memo about Pecos Bill.

Vocabulary

- tale
- frontier
- hero
- heroine
- exaggerate
- deeds
- settler
- tradition

To: *The East Coast Gazette*

From: Gil Ibel, Gazette Staff

Subject: Pecos Bill Story

Last week I took a stagecoach to the Kansas

_____. Since arriving, I have spoken to

every _____ in town, but have had no

luck in getting an interview with Pecos Bill. However, I

think I may have heard about every one of the amazing

_____ he has ever done. It seems the

folks around here have a _____ of gather-

ing daily to swap Pecos Bill stories. He is unlike any other

_____ or _____ I have

ever written about. At yesterday's meeting, I heard one

_____ about how Bill was raised by coyotes

and another about how he came to use a rattlesnake as a

whip. Then someone told me he'd left town on a cyclone

headed for Arizona or Wyoming. I'm still not sure how to

find him, but I do not _____ when I say that

this is the best story I have ever followed!

Name _____

Tackle a Tall Tale

Tale _____

Character, Setting, Plot
Main Character(s)
Setting
Plot: Important Events in the Tale
Tall Tale Exaggeration
Exaggerated Character Traits
Exaggerated or Impossible Setting Elements
Exaggerated or Impossible Actions or Events
Factual Details

For me, the funniest part of this tall tale was _____

_____

Name _____

That Could Never Happen!

Each of the four selections in *Focus on Tall Tales* contains at least one exaggerated event. Write the event after each story title.

Paul Bunyan, the Mightiest Logger of Them All

_____

_____

John Henry Races the Steam Drill

_____

_____

Sally Ann Thunder Ann Whirlwind

_____

_____

February

_____

_____

Name _____

You'll Never Believe Whom I Just Met.

Think about characters you might find in a tall tale. Describe five tall tale characters by completing each sentence with an exaggeration.

1. This character is so tall that

_____

_____

2. This character is so loud that

_____

_____

3. This character is so old that

_____

_____

4. This character is so fast that

_____

_____

_____

5. This character is so strong that

_____

_____

Name _____

Tackle Another Tall Tale

Tale _____

Character, Setting, Plot
Main Character(s)
Setting
Plot: Important Events in the Tale
Tall Tale Exaggeration
Exaggerated Character Traits
Exaggerated or Impossible Setting Elements
Exaggerated or Impossible Actions or Events
Factual Details

For me, the funniest part of this tall tale was _____

_____

Name _____

Growing Words from their Roots

Vis and *vid* are word roots. They have meaning, but are words by themselves. The Latin word roots *vis* and *vid* mean "to see."

television   videotape   supervision

Complete each sentence. Build a word containing the root *vis* or *vid*.

vis + ion	re + vis + e
e + vid + ent	pro + vid + e
vis + or	in + vis + ible

1. Max put on his _____ because the sun was in his eyes.

2. We missed the turn because the road sign was almost _____ in the darkness.

3. When Hank slowly shuffled into class with his head down, it was _____ that he had not done his homework.

4. The factory has been without power for two days, but the new generator they bought will _____ enough energy.

5. The famous actor disliked the original script, so the writer was brought in to make a major _____.

Now write sentences using four of the words you constructed.

_____

_____

_____

_____

Name _____

Long to Short

A long vowel sound may be spelled the same as a short vowel sound in words that are related in meaning.

    long vowel sound: divide

    short vowel sound: division

Write a pair of related Spelling Words in each row. Write each word under the heading that shows whether the common vowel letter or letters have a long or a short vowel sound. Underline the vowel letter or letters that are common in both words.

Spelling Words

1. steal
2. stealth
3. cave
4. cavity
5. wise
6. wisdom
7. deal
8. dealt
9. athlete
10. athletic
11. crime
12. criminal
13. breathe
14. breath
15. wild
16. wilderness
17. shade
18. shadow
19. revise
20. revision

Long Vowel Sound	Short Vowel Sound
_____	_____
_____	_____
_____	_____
_____	_____
_____	_____
_____	_____
_____	_____
_____	_____
_____	_____
_____	_____

Name _____

Spelling Spree

Letter Swap Write a Spelling Word by changing the underlined letter or letters to one or more different letters.

1. rev<u>i</u>ve _____

2. <u>d</u>eath _____

3. sha<u>p</u>e _____

4. <u>m</u>ild _____

5. shal<u>l</u>ow _____

6. wi<u>f</u>e _____

7. stea<u>m</u> _____

8. <u>w</u>ave _____

9. <u>m</u>eal _____

10. <u>w</u>ealth _____

Analogies An analogy compares word pairs that are related in the same way. An analogy might use pairs of opposites or pairs of synonyms, or it might show word pairs that name a category and an item in that category. Write the Spelling Word that completes each analogy.

> **Opposites:** *Hot* is to *cold* as *last* is to *first.*
> **Category and item:** *Hammer* is to *tool* as *peach* is to *fruit.*

11. *Building* is to *city* as *forest* is to _____.

12. *Dentist* is to *doctor* as *burglar* is to _____.

13. *Sadness* is to *joy* as *foolishness* is to _____.

14. *Iron* is to *rust* as *tooth* is to _____.

15. *Proofread* is to *correction* as *edit* is to _____.

Spelling Words

1. steal
2. stealth
3. cave
4. cavity
5. wise
6. wisdom
7. deal
8. dealt
9. athlete
10. athletic
11. crime
12. criminal
13. breathe
14. breath
15. wild
16. wilderness
17. shade
18. shadow
19. revise
20. revision

Name _____

Proofreading and Writing

Proofreading Circle the five misspelled Spelling Words in this paragraph from a tall tale. Then write each word correctly.

Back in the Old West, Burl Redwood was known far and wide as the most atheletic man who ever walked this planet. He could outrun, outjump, outride, outfight, outwrestle—just plain outdo anyone or anything. With great stealth Burl could sneak up on a grizzly bear, breeth down its neck, and then chase it for miles through the wilderness until the bear dropped from exhaustion. When Burl had a problem, he delt with it by holding a contest, which he always won.

One time, though, Burl committed a crim in a town policed by Wiley Wunn. That wise sheriff was eager to match wits with the famous athleet.

1. steal
2. stealth
3. cave
4. cavity
5. wise
6. wisdom
7. deal
8. dealt
9. athlete
10. athletic
11. crime
12. criminal
13. breathe
14. breath
15. wild
16. wilderness
17. shade
18. shadow
19. revise
20. revision

1. _____
2. _____
3. _____
4. _____
5. _____

Make a Wanted Poster Think of a tall tale character whose special abilities might get him or her in trouble. Think about the character's abilities and what problems they might cause.

On a separate sheet of paper, create a wanted poster for your character. List the character's abilities and reasons why he or she is wanted. Use Spelling Words from the list.

Name _____

Informally Speaking

Tom has written a letter to Marissa, who lives in France. She doesn't
know American slang very well and may not understand what Tom is
talking about! Help make his letter easier to understand. Replace each
underlined slang word or phrase with a proper word or phrase that means
the same thing. Write the new word or words on the line that has the
same number.

Dear Marissa,

    I'm psyched to come visit you this summer. Paris sounds so cool,
<u>1</u> ... <u>2</u>
and you're a real pal to invite me. My old man says he's been to France
<u>3</u> ... <u>4</u>
with my mom. He told me it's just as nice as it looks in the French flicks
<u>5</u>
we rented at the video store. I've been watching a French-language show
on the tube so I can learn a few words and phrases. I figure if I cram for
<u>6</u> ... <u>7</u>
two weeks, I'll know how say hello and goodbye, and how to order some
of that famous French chow. I'm planning to pig out the whole time! If I
<u>8</u> ... <u>9</u>
croak after eating too many French pastries, no sweat!
<u>10</u> ... <u>11</u>
    Okay, I've got to hop on my wheels and deliver the local rag now,
<u>12</u> ... <u>13</u>
so I can earn some greenbacks for the trip. Talk to you soon!
<u>14</u>

Your friend,

Tom

1. _____   8. _____

2. _____   9. _____

3. _____   10. _____

4. _____   11. _____

5. _____   12. _____

6. _____   13. _____

7. _____   14. _____

Name _____

A Hairy Tale

Using Sentence Variety Use different types of sentences to make your writing more interesting and smooth to read. Use declarative, interrogative, imperative, or exclamatory sentences. Use compound sentences or sentences with compound subjects or compound predicates.

Rewrite these paragraphs describing a tall tale character. Change five sentences to introduce more sentence variety.

Maybe you have heard tales about Hairy Harry. Harry was born with long hair wrapped around him like a cocoon. His parents tied it in a ponytail. It dragged behind him like a king's robe for more than twenty feet.

Harry soon learned that he could use that hair like an extra arm. One time Harry fell down an old well. His sister, Harriet, fell in, too. Harry flipped his hair out of that well. He wrapped it around a tree trunk. Harriet climbed up his hair. Then Harry climbed up his hair. They were out of that well lickety-split.

_____

_____

_____

_____

_____

_____

_____

_____

Name _____

Name a Noun

Appositives An appositive is a phrase that includes a noun that tells more about another noun in the same sentence. Use commas to set off an appositive.

Sally Ann Thunder Ann Whirlwind, the title character, was amazing.

Rewrite each sentence. Add the phrase from the box that tells more about the underlined noun. Use commas correctly.

an alligator's skin
an eagle's nest
a muddy swamp
a riverboat man
his rival

1. <u>Mike Fink</u> wanted to play a mean trick.

_____

_____

2. He was tired of hearing <u>Davy Crockett</u> praise Sally.

_____

_____

3. Mike decided to wear a <u>disguise</u>.

_____

_____

4. Sally gave him a whack, and he landed in an uncomfortable <u>place</u>.

_____

_____

5. Sally wore her favorite hat to meet Davy.

_____

_____

Counselor Wanted

Using Commas with Appositives Use commas to set off an appositive. If an appositive ends a sentence, it is followed by only the end mark.

Use proofreading marks to correct ten errors in punctuation and capitalization in this job advertisement.

Example: this job, a real opportunity, looks interesting

A great opportunity awaits you Camp Timberlake a wilderness retreat for boys and girls in Minnesota has an opening for a junior counselor. Do you love the sound of the wind and the smell of campfires. Help our young campers children from large cities learn about and appreciate the sights, sounds, and smells of the outdoors. Lead hikes and campfire songs tell and create tall tales? We offer good pay and plenty of fun. Apply at our office the first red cabin.

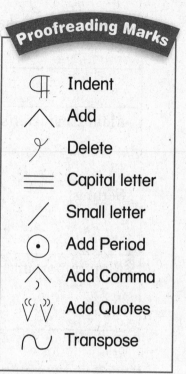

Proofreading Marks

⊓	Indent
∧	Add
⅊	Delete
═	Capital letter
/	Small letter
⊙	Add Period
∧	Add Comma
᭡᭡	Add Quotes
∽	Transpose

Name _____

Planning a Tall Tale

Use the Chart to help plan your tall tale.

Character, Setting, Plot
Main Character(s)
Setting
Plot: Important Events in the Tale

Tall Tale Exaggeration
Exaggerated Character Traits
Exaggerated or Impossible Setting Elements
Exaggerated or Impossible Actions or Events
Realistic Details

Name _____

Using Exact Nouns

Choose an exact noun from the box to replace each underlined vague noun or noun phrase. Write your answers on the lines below.

Anna-Hanna-Diana was the most stunning gymnast in (1) <u>the continent</u>. When she jumped onto the balance beam, (2) <u>people</u> in the bleachers watched in awe. She did one (3) <u>thing</u> after another and then ended by turning somersaults as she leapt off. If you counted, you'd see she did (4) <u>lots</u> of them in midair.

One day Anna-Hanna-Diana heard that a big (5) <u>event</u> was going on in (6) <u>a state</u>. It started that very day. She said, "I'm going!"

Her mother said, "How will you get there? We're in New York! No (7) <u>transportation</u> can get you there quickly enough."

Well, Anna-Hanna-Diana got there on time. It took a fierce set of cross-country back flips to get her to (8) <u>that city</u> but she arrived in only a (9) <u>short time</u>. She won every (10) <u>item</u> at the meet, as usual.

1. _____   6. _____
2. _____   7. _____
3. _____   8. _____
4. _____   9. _____
5. _____   10. _____

Exact Nouns

half-hour	fifty-five
Tucson	North America
airplane	fans
trophy	Arizona
cartwheel	gymnastics meet

Name _____

Give It All You've Got

How do the characters in this theme "give their all"? After reading each selection, answer the questions to complete the chart.

	Michelle Kwan: Heart of a Champion	La Bamba
What kind of writing is the selection an example of?		
What traits does the main character have? What actions or achievements help reveal those traits?		
Why does this selection belong in a theme called Give It All You've Got?		
What advice might the main character give to others?		

Name _____

Give It All You've Got

	Mae Jemison: Space Scientist	The Fear Place
What kind of writing is the selection an example of?		
What traits does the main character have? What actions or achievements help reveal those traits?		
Why does this selection belong in a theme called *Give It All You've Got*?		
What advice might the main character give to others?		

What have you learned in this theme about facing challenges?

_____

_____

Name _____

Top Marks

Read the word in each box from *Michelle Kwan: Heart of a Champion*. Write a word from the list that is related in meaning. Then use a dictionary to check if you were right.

pressure	required
_____	_____

presentations	audience
_____	_____

elements	artistic
_____	_____

judges	amateur
_____	_____

technical	compete
_____	_____

Vocabulary

demonstrations
officials
perform
components
stress
elegant
nonprofessional
skilled
specified
spectators

Name _____

Is That a Fact?

Passage	Fact or Opinion?	How I Can Tell
Page 139, paragraph 1: "I thought I was ready to become a Senior skater, at the age of twelve."		
Page 140, paragraph 5: "Frank is one of the greatest coaches in the world."		
Page 144, paragraph 6: "The judges look for many required elements in a program."		
Page 146, paragraph 3: "Elvis Stojko...does quadruple/triple combinations."		
Page 147, paragraph 1: "Most elite skaters have three forty-five-minute-long practice sessions on the ice every day . . ."		
Page 150, paragraph 4: "And you can never forget how important school is."		

Name _____

A Figure Skater's Trading Card

What if figure skaters were featured on trading cards as baseball players are? Complete the fact sheet so it gives vital information about Michelle Kwan. Then use the facts to write a paragraph that might appear on the back of a Michelle Kwan trading card.

FACT SHEET

Who Michelle Kwan is:

_____

Who her coach was:

_____

What she was especially good at when she was young:

_____

Age at which she became a Senior skater:

_____

How she had to improve in order to compete as a Senior skater:

_____

_____

_____

Her world records (see page 151):

_____

Two pieces of advice she might give other young athletes:

1. _____

2. _____

Michelle Kwan: Figure Skater

Name _____

Is That a Fact?

Read the following passage. Then answer the questions on page 99.

A Track Legend

Wilma Rudolph was perhaps the greatest female track athlete of her time. She was the first American woman to win three gold medals in a single Olympics. She also received many honors, including the Sullivan Award as the country's top amateur athlete, and a place in the Women's Sports Hall of Fame, the Black Sports Hall of Fame, and the United States Olympic Hall of Fame.

Rudolph achieved success despite great personal obstacles. As a child, she was stricken with polio, pneumonia, and scarlet fever. Some doctors said she would never walk. Yet no one could have been more determined to beat the odds. After years of physical therapy, Rudolph put aside her leg brace at age eleven and went on to become a great athlete in high school and college.

At the 1960 Olympic Games, Rudolph was the star of the American team. She won gold medals and set world records in the 100-meter dash, the 200-meter dash, and the 400-meter relay.

Rudolph later became a coach and a teacher. She also wrote a book about her life that was made into a movie. There has never been an American athlete who overcame more obstacles in life than Wilma Rudolph. She should be an inspiration to all Americans, and to athletes everywhere.

Name _____

Is That a Fact? continued

Answer these questions about the passage on page 98.

1. What opinion about Wilma Rudolph does the author give in the first paragraph? Write the sentence that states the opinion.

   _____

   _____

2. Which words in this sentence show that the statement is an opinion and not a fact?

   _____

3. Which sentence from the second paragraph contains no opinions?

   _____

   _____

4. The third paragraph contains one opinion and several facts. Write them here.

   Opinion: _____

   _____

   Facts: _____

   _____

5. Reread the last paragraph to find two facts and two opinions. Write them here.

   Opinion: _____

   _____

   Facts: _____

   _____

Name _____

Compound Creativity

Read the pairs of sentences. Identify the compound word in the first sentence, and write the words it is made from.

1. Even when my piano recital didn't go well, I believed in myself.

   _____ + _____

2. Jen will do whatever it takes to make the soccer team.

   _____ + _____

3. Throughout the school year, I use the gym as often as I can.

   _____ + _____

4. I have to do my homework before I can go biking with my friends.

   _____ + _____

5. Philip spoke loudly from the stage so that everybody in the
   auditorium could hear him.

   _____ + _____

Word Chain **Play a compound word game. Start with a compound word. Use either of the words in it to form a new compound word. Then use part of the new word to form another compound. Keep your word chain going as long as you can.**

Example: anymore ⟶ anyway ⟶ freeway ⟶ wayside ⟶ ?

Name _____

Compound Words

A **compound word** is made up of two or more smaller words. To spell a compound word correctly, you must remember if it is written as one word, as a hyphenated word, or as separate words.

wheel + chair = wheelchair **up + to + date** = up-to-date

first + aid = first aid

Write each Spelling Word under the heading that tells how the compound word is written.

One Word

_____ _____
_____ _____
_____ _____
_____ _____
_____ _____
_____ _____
_____ _____

With a Hyphen   ### Separate Words

_____ _____
_____ _____

Name _____

Spelling Spree

Exchanging Word Parts Write the Spelling Word that has one of the parts in each compound word below.

1. wildfire   _____

2. dateline   _____

3. grandstand   _____

4. sales tax   _____

5. evergreen   _____

6. wayside   _____

7. turnover   _____

8. holdup   _____

Clue Addition Add the clues to create a Spelling Word.

9. large boat + play area =

10. comes before second + assist =

11. "Hooray!" + person in charge =

12. try out + hollow cylinder =

13. container made of twigs + sphere =

14. not night + what a watch measures =

15. circular frame with spokes + piece of furniture =

9. _____

10. _____

11. _____

12. _____

13. _____

14. _____

15. _____

Spelling Words

1. basketball
2. wheelchair
3. cheerleader
4. newscast
5. weekend
6. everybody
7. up-to-date
8. grandparent
9. first aid
10. wildlife
11. highway
12. daytime
13. whoever
14. test tube
15. turnpike
16. shipyard
17. homemade
18. household
19. salesperson
20. brother-in-law

Name _____

Proofreading and Writing

Proofreading Circle the five misspelled Spelling Words in this transcript of a television news report. Then write each word correctly.

To end tonight's newskast, we have a story about a local girl who made good. Debbie Martin, who started skating years ago on a pair of homemad skates, is going to the Junior Nationals. Debbie's parents, older sister, and brother-in-lor will accompany her to Seattle. For years, they have watched Debbie practice on the family's basketball court, which her father flooded in winter and allowed to freeze over. This week-end they will watch her in a world-class arena. We know that everbody in town will be rooting for Debbie!

1. _____

2. _____

3. _____

4. _____

5. _____

Spelling Words

1. basketball
2. wheelchair
3. cheerleader
4. newscast
5. weekend
6. everybody
7. up-to-date
8. grandparent
9. first aid
10. wildlife
11. highway
12. daytime
13. whoever
14. test tube
15. turnpike
16. shipyard
17. homemade
18. household
19. salesperson
20. brother-in-law

Write a Comparison and Contrast Think of a sport you enjoy playing or watching. Does it have anything in common with figure skating? How is it different from figure skating?

On a separate piece of paper, write a paragraph in which you compare and contrast two sports. Use Spelling Words from the list.

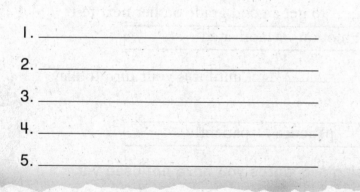

Name _____

Word Family Matters

Decide which word best completes each sentence. Write the word in the blank.

1. When he realized that he had missed the team tryouts, Todd

   turned red with _____

furious   fury   infuriate

2. Twenty school bands besides ours were entered in this year's

   state _____.

compete   competition   competitive

3. Vanilla ice cream with fudge sauce is a dessert I find

   _____.

irresistible   resistance   resist

4. Because the top math student receives a prize, my sister is

   _____ to get a good grade on her next test.

move   motion   motivated

5. Please wait _____ until it is your turn to play

   the computer game.

impatient   patience   patiently

Now write two sentences, using two words you have not used yet.

6. _____

   _____

7. _____

   _____

Name _____

Champion Michelle

Common and Proper Nouns A **common noun** names any person, place, or thing. A **proper noun** names a particular person, place, or thing. Each important word in a proper noun begins with a capital letter.

> We met at the **statue**. *statue:* common noun
> We met at the **Statue of Liberty**. *Statue of Liberty:* proper noun
> **Coach Boe** taught me how to skate. *Coach Boe:* proper noun
> A **coach** taught me how to skate. *coach:* common noun
> She is from another **state**. *state:* common noun
> She is from **California**. *California:* proper noun

Copy the nouns from the following sentences into the proper columns below. When you rewrite a proper noun, be sure to capitalize correctly.

1. debbie went to the skating rink on saturday.
2. In the winter, the pond is frozen.
3. miguel is fast when he puts on his skates.
4. I competed in the race at valley middle school.
5. Have you ever skated at rockefeller center?

Common Nouns

_____

_____

_____

_____

Proper Nouns

_____

_____

_____

_____

Name _____

The People's Favorite

Singular and Possessive Nouns A **possessive noun** shows ownership or possession. To form a singular possessive noun, add an apostrophe and -s ('s). To form a plural possessive noun, add an apostrophe (') if the noun ends with s. Otherwise, add an apostrophe and -s ('s).

Singular	Singular Possessive	Plural	Plural Possessive
cat	cat's	cats	cats'
country	country's	countries	countries'
Jones	Jones's	Joneses	Joneses'
woman	woman's	women	women's
mouse	mouse's	mice	mice's

Fill in the blank in each sentence below with the possessive form of the noun in parentheses. Write an S on the line at the end of the sentence if you wrote a singular possessive noun. Write a P on the line if you wrote a plural possessive noun.

1. Our (school) _____ skating club

   sponsored a citywide competition. ___

2. The fifth grade (classes) _____

   skaters were great. ___

3. The first event was the (seniors) _____

   short program. ___

4. The (competition) _____ rules were

   strict. ___

5. The audience's favorite event was the (children)

   _____ competition. ___

Name _____

My Friend's Skating Pond

Writing Possessive Phrases It is easy to make a mistake when forming the possessive of a plural or a singular noun. Therefore, when you proofread, pay special attention to possessive nouns.

Chris in Maine wants to send this e-mail message to Joann in Florida. Proofread the message for errors in possessive nouns. Write the correct possessive forms above the line, as shown.

friends'
Example: My two friend's reports are about hockey.
                        ^

To: joann@tropics.net
From: cwm@frozennorth.com
Re: Ice and Snow

Hi Joann!

I have been ice-skating on my familys pond. The

pond froze solid last week. It is safe to skate on it

now. Last evening, Toms family and my family skated

on the pond. Our families dogs played in the snow.

The dogs tails never stopped wagging. They enjoyed

this winters snow as much as we did!

Chris

Writing an Announcement

How can you find out when and where Michelle Kwan is going to skate in a competition or perform in an exhibition? You might read an announcement on a bulletin board or in a newsletter, or you might hear one on the radio or TV. An **announcement** is a short speech or notice that gives important information about an event.

Fill in the chart below with details about an upcoming skating performance by Michelle Kwan or some other sporting event.

Date
Time
Place
Cost
Details about the program

Now write your announcement on a separate sheet of paper. State the purpose of the announcement at the very beginning. Then provide information that answers these questions: *who? what? where? when? why? how?* **and** *how much?* **Be sure to include the exact date, time, location, and cost of the event as well as other details about the program. Use clear, interesting, and friendly language that the audience will understand.**

Name _____

Ordering Important Information

A careful writer makes sure that the information in an announcement is complete and presented in a clear order. Sequence words, such as *first*, *next*, and *last*, help clarify the order of events and call attention to what is most important.

Somehow, this announcement has gotten scrambled. Reorder the sentences so that the announcement follows the sequence of events. Pay attention to sequence words that give clues to the order of the sentences. Then write the revised announcement on the lines below.

After the match, a victory party will be held in the cafeteria. Game time is 3 P.M. Following the pep rally, the Bloomington Wildcats will play against the Forest Lane Eagles for the regional championship at O'Neill Field. During the rally, Coach Strauss will introduce all of the players and hand out free T-shirts and banners. There will be a pre-game pep rally tomorrow at 2:20 in the gym before the most important soccer match of the season. Go Wildcats!

_____

_____

_____

_____

_____

_____

Name _____

Revising Your Personal Essay

Reread your personal essay. Put a checkmark in the box for each sentence that describes your paper. Use this page to help you revise.

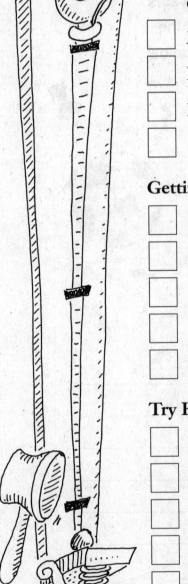

Rings the Bell

☐ I focused on one opinion and supported it with reasons and details.

☐ My reasons and details are organized in paragraphs.

☐ I wrote a strong introduction and a strong conclusion.

☐ I used precise words that make my feelings clear.

☐ Sentences flow smoothly. There are few mistakes.

Getting Stronger

☐ I focused on one opinion, but I need more reasons and details.

☐ My paragraphs are somewhat disorganized.

☐ My introduction and conclusion could be stronger.

☐ The words I chose don't always make my feelings clear.

☐ Some sentences are choppy. There are a few mistakes.

Try Harder

☐ I did not focus on one opinion. There are few reasons and details.

☐ My paper is just a list of thoughts.

☐ My introduction or conclusion are missing.

☐ Word choice is bland. My essay sounds flat.

☐ Most sentences are choppy. There are many mistakes.

Name _____

Using Possessive Nouns

► Possessive nouns show ownership.

► To form the possessive of a singular noun add an apostrophe and *s*.

► To form the possessive case of a plural noun ending in *s*, add just an apostrophe.

Rewrite each phrase, using a possessive noun. Then use the new phrase in a sentence of your own.

1. the music of the composer _____

_____

2. the skill of the musicians _____

_____

3. the authority of the conductor _____

_____

4. the hush of the spectators _____

_____

5. the sore throat of the actress _____

_____

6. the big chance for the understudy _____

_____

7. the groan of the audience _____

_____

8. the surprise of the critics _____

_____

Name _____

Spelling Words

Look for familiar spelling patterns to help you remember how to spell the Spelling Words on this page. Think carefully about the parts that you find hard to spell in each word.

Write the missing letters in the Spelling Words below.

1. w _____ _____ _____ d

2. w _____ _____ _____ dn't

3. clo _____ _____ _____ _____

4. happ _____ _____ _____ _____

5. som _____ one

6. sometim _____ _____

7. diff _____ r _____ nt

8. an _____ ther

9. w _____ _____ _____ d

10. eig _____ _____ _____

11. c _____ _____ ing

12. g _____ _____ _____ ing

13. g _____ ing

14. st _____ _____ _____ ed

15. h _____ _____ _____

Study List On a separate piece of paper, write each Spelling Word.
Check your spelling against the words on the list.

Name _____

Spelling Spree

Find a Rhyme **For each sentence write a Spelling Word that rhymes with the underlined word and makes sense in the sentence.**

1. The band _____ playing when the singer <u>dropped</u> his microphone.
2. When Alison <u>peered</u> out the window, she saw a _____ looking bird.
3. If my sweatshirt had a <u>hood</u>, I _____ definitely wear it on a day like this.
4. A <u>humming</u> sound was _____ from the car's engine.
5. We're _____ to the store after you finish <u>mowing</u> the lawn.
6. You <u>shouldn't</u> treat anyone in a way you _____ want to be treated yourself.
7. You have nothing to <u>fear</u> _____.

Spelling Words

1. would
2. wouldn't
3. clothes
4. happened
5. someone
6. sometimes
7. different
8. another
9. weird
10. eighth
11. coming
12. getting
13. going
14. stopped
15. here

1. _____   5. _____
2. _____   6. _____
3. _____   7. _____
4. _____

Finding Words **Each word below is hidden in a Spelling Word. Write the Spelling Word.**

8. pen
9. on
10. eight
11. tin
12. cloth
13. not
14. met
15. rent

8. _____
9. _____
10. _____   13. _____
11. _____   14. _____
12. _____   15. _____

I'm *letting* her stay ahead of me until she starts *getting* tired.

Name _____

Proofreading and Writing

Proofreading Circle the five misspelled Spelling Words in this certificate. Then write each word correctly.

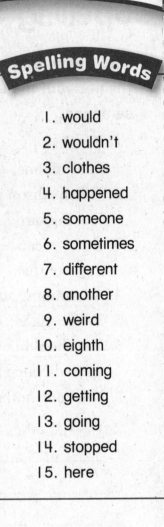

Certificate of Effort

This is to certify that Eduardo Díaz gave it all he had in the four hundred meter race held on the eightth day of May of this year. Just as the runners were geting to the first turn, Eduardo fell. (No one is sure just how it happenned.) He could easily have stoped running there. Instead, he got back up, kept goeing, and finished the race. We are proud to recognize him here for his extraordinary effort.

1. would
2. wouldn't
3. clothes
4. happened
5. someone
6. sometimes
7. different
8. another
9. weird
10. eighth
11. coming
12. getting
13. going
14. stopped
15. here

1. _____   4. _____

2. _____   5. _____

3. _____

━━━━ **Writing Headlines** Write four headlines for newspaper stories about people who gave it all they had. The headlines can be about people in the theme's selections, can be about people you know of from somewhere else, or can be completely made up. Include a Spelling Word in each headline.

Name _____

What a Performance!

Words are missing in the sentences. Fill each blank with a word or words from the box.

1. If you are the only one on stage, you are in the _____ .

2. If you are good at something, you have _____ .

3. If you buy an old record with one song on each side, you become the owner of a _____ .

4. If you have agreed to help, you have _____ .

5. If you act without speaking, you _____ .

6. If you perform for the first time, you make your _____ .

7. If you go to practice a play, you attend a _____ .

8. If you forget your lines during a play, you may feel _____ .

9. If you please the audience, you may hear _____ .

10. If you perform with a partner, you are part of a _____ .

Name _____

Talent Report

Fill in the story map with information from the selection.

Characters	Setting
_____ _____	_____ _____

Plot

Events

1. _____
   _____

2. _____
   _____

3. _____
   _____

4. _____
   _____

Problem

5. _____
   _____

Solution

6. _____
   _____
   _____

Name _____

Manuel's Journal

Suppose Manuel wrote about the talent show in his journal. Finish each sentence to show what he might have said about his performance.

September _____, _____
    (today's date)   (year)

I can't believe I survived the talent show. Here's how it happened. I'd volunteered to _____
_____. Two things happened at rehearsal that should have made me nervous. First, Mr. Roybal's record player speed _____. Then, when Benny blew his trumpet, I _____.

On the night of the show, I had to wait for my turn onstage. A lot of other kids performed before me. As I watched them, I _____. Finally it was my turn. At first, _____.

Then, suddenly, something awful happened: _____
_____

I didn't know what to do, so I _____
_____. As I left the stage, I
_____.

Here's the funny thing. After the performance _____
_____

I couldn't believe that _____.

Name _____

A Class Act

Read the story. Then complete the activity on page 119.

Horsing Around

Every year, the fifth grade classes held a big softball game and talent show. This year, Amy and Carmen decided to enter the talent show. Since their team was the Mustangs, the girls decided to dance in a horse costume. Amy would be the front half and Carmen the back half.

They spent an entire weekend making a papier-mâché horse's head. Carmen's dad sewed the body from fleecy brown cloth. The girls made the mane and tail out of thick black yarn. Amy's mom helped them learn a dance to a song called "Plains Pony."

At last it was the day of the show. But as the girls nervously galloped onto the softball diamond, they heard giggling from the audience. Someone called, "Hey, Horsey! You forgot something!" Carmen gasped, "Oh, no!" Peeking out from the horse's head, Amy saw something black near home plate. Their tail!

"What will we do?" Carmen whispered. Amy replied, "We'll pretend we planned it this way!" The next time they passed home plate, they danced around the tail and Amy snatched it up. Then she and Carmen danced backwards off the field, shaking their hooves to the music as Amy waved goodbye with the tail. The audience applauded noisily, screaming with laughter.

Name _____

A Class Act continued

Fill in the story map so it sums up the story on page 118. Write the characters' names, the setting, and the events that make up the plot.

Main Characters	**Setting** (time and place)
_____	_____

Plot

_____

_____

_____

_____

_____

Problem

_____

_____

_____

Solution

_____

_____

_____

Name _____

Record Roots

Some words in the box contain the word root *spec*. Others contain the root *opt*. Write the words that match each clue. Then write each numbered letter in the space with the matching number to find a message.

inspector

optician

optometry

respect

spectacle

suspect

1. a person who makes or sells eyeglasses

__ __ __ __ __ __ __ __
    9   6

2. to look up to or regard highly

__ __ __ __ __ __ __
 7

3. a remarkable or impressive sight

__ __ __ __ __ __ __ __ __
  3   5

4. the profession of examining a person's vision

__ __ __ __ __ __ __ __ __
               10

5. to look upon someone as guilty without proof

__ __ __ __ __ __ __
  4 1

6. a person who examines something closely and carefully

__ __ __ __ __ __ __ __ __
 8   2

Manuel gained a lot of __ __ __ __ __ __ __ __ __ __ __ after his performance.
        1 2 3 4 5 6 7 8 9 10

Name _____

The /ou/, /ô/, and /oi/ Sounds

When you hear the /ou/, the /ô/, and the /oi/ sounds, think of these patterns:

/ou/ *ou, ow* **ou**nce, t**ow**er

/ô/ *aw, au, a* before *l* cl**aw**, p**au**se, b**al**d

/oi/ *oi, oy* m**oi**st, l**oy**al

Remember that the patterns *ou*, *au*, and *oi* are usually followed by a consonant sound.

Write each Spelling Word under its vowel sound.

Spelling Words

1. hawk
2. claw
3. bald
4. tower
5. halt
6. prowl
7. loyal
8. pause
9. moist
10. ounce
11. launch
12. royal
13. scowl
14. haunt
15. noisy
16. coward
17. fawn
18. thousand
19. drown
20. fault

/ou/ Sound

_____

_____

_____

_____

_____

_____

_____

/ô/ Sound

_____

_____

_____

_____

_____

_____

_____

_____

/oi/ Sound

_____

_____

_____

_____

Name _____

Spelling Spree

Contrast Clues The second part of each clue contrasts with the first part. Write a Spelling Word after each clue.

1. not hairy, but _____

2. not a traitor, but _____

3. not a smile, but a _____

4. not to dock, but to _____

5. not an adult deer, but a _____

6. not a pound, but an _____

7. not a sparrow, but a _____

8. not lowly or common, but _____

9. not quiet, but _____

10. not to move about openly, but to _____

Finding Words Each word below is hidden in a Spelling Word. Write the Spelling Words that contain these words.

11. aunt _____

12. tow _____

13. sand _____

14. law _____

15. use _____

Spelling Words

1. hawk
2. claw
3. bald
4. tower
5. halt
6. prowl
7. loyal
8. pause
9. moist
10. ounce
11. launch
12. royal
13. scowl
14. haunt
15. noisy
16. coward
17. fawn
18. thousand
19. drown
20. fault

Proofreading and Writing

Circle the five misspelled Spelling Words in this e-mail that Manuel might have sent. Then write each word correctly.

| File | Edit | View | Toolbox | Help | ✉ |

To: Grandma

From: Manuel

Subject: Talent Show

The show turned out okay, but I was pretty nervous beforehand. My hands were moyst with sweat. I'm no cowerd, though. I went out and started my act. Then the record stuck, and I had to sing the same words over and over. It was Benny's falt for making me scratch the record. When the music finally came to a hault, I ran offstage. I felt awful! At the end of the show, though, I got a round of applause noisy enough to droun out the names of the other acts. Nobody was more surprised than I was!

1. _____   4. _____

2. _____   5. _____

3. _____

1. hawk
2. claw
3. bald
4. tower
5. halt
6. prowl
7. loyal
8. pause
9. moist
10. ounce
11. launch
12. royal
13. scowl
14. haunt
15. noisy
16. coward
17. fawn
18. thousand
19. drown
20. fault

✏── Write an Announcement Suppose that Manuel decided to give another performance of "La Bamba." How would you go about advertising it? What information would you need to include? How would you describe his act?

On a separate piece of paper, write an announcement for this repeat performance. Use Spelling Words from the list.

Name _____

Mixed Meanings

Read the definitions of each word. Then write one or two sentences that use different meanings of each word.

fall (fôl) *v.* **fell, fallen, falling, falls. 1.** To drop or come down. **2.** To suffer defeat or capture. **3.** *n.* The season of the year occurring between summer and winter.

1. _____

_____

hand (hănd) *n.* **1.** The part of the arm below the wrist. **2.** A round of applause. *v.* To give or pass with the hands; transmit.

2. _____

_____

stage (stāj) *n.* **1.** A raised platform, especially one in a theater on which entertainers perform. **2.** A level or step in a process. *v.* To produce or direct a performance.

3. _____

_____

step (stĕp) *n.* **1.** The movement of raising one foot and putting it down. **2.** An action taken to achieve a goal. *v.* To press the foot down or against.

4. _____

_____

stick (stĭk) *n.* A long slender piece of wood. *v.* **1.** To fasten or attach, as with a pin or nail. **2.** To become fixed and unable to move.

5. _____

Name _____

Mary Sings and Puppets Move

Action Verbs An **action verb** tells what the subject does or did. It is the main word in the complete predicate.

The performers **bowed** to the audience.

action verb

Underline the action verb in each of the following sentences.

1. Martin and Mary built a small theater for their puppet show.

2. Martin's father cut the wood for them.

3. Martin painted designs on the wooden theater.

4. Mary picked a song for their show.

5. On the night of the show, Martin watches the audience.

6. The audience claps for the tap dancer.

7. Martin and Mary carry their puppets on stage.

8. The puppets dance to the music.

9. The puppeteers wait for applause.

10. The crowd cheers!

Name _____

He Gave a Speech

Direct Objects A **direct object** is a noun or pronoun in a predicate that receives the action of the verb. It answers the question *What?* or *Whom?*

> The dancer tied his **shoes.**
>
> The dancer tied *what?* His shoes. Therefore, *shoes* is the direct object.

Underline the action verb and circle the direct object in each sentence below.

1. Mr. Bruno needed a volunteer to give a speech.

2. Sydney raised his hand.

3. Mr. Bruno thanked him for volunteering.

4. Sydney nervously shuffled his notes.

5. Then he cleared his throat.

6. He projected his voice throughout the room.

7. Susan heard his words in the back of the classroom.

8. After the speech, Mario asked a question of Sydney.

9. Sydney answered the query politely.

10. Then Sydney set his notes down.

Name _____

She Wrote and I Scribbled

Using Exact Verbs Your writing will be more vivid if you use action verbs that tell exactly what the subject of the sentence is doing. Look at the two sentences below. Which verb gives you a better idea of how Sandy made her way across the stage?

Sandy **moved** across the stage.

Sandy **twirled** across the stage.

Pat is writing a review of the class play for the school newspaper. Replace each underlined verb with a more exact one. Choose from among the verbs in the box.

stomped
stumbled
shouted
fumbled
scribbled

Last night I saw the class play *Ramshackle Inn*. There were five main

characters. The innkeeper was a loud man with a beard. When he said his

lines, others onstage covered their ears. The brother was clumsy. He

walked back and forth across the stage. His rude and angry sister walked

up and down the stairs. The reporter wrote constantly in his pad. The

inept police officer was the funniest character of all. She played with her

radio, trying to get it to work. The plot of this play was silly, but the

actors were fun to watch.

Name _____

Writing a Summary

If you were asked to summarize "La Bamba," you would probably tell who performed in the talent show and what happened during the performances. A **summary** is a brief account of a story or selection. Writing a summary is a good way to share what a story is about and to recall main events and characters.

Choose a selection you have read, such as *Earthquake Terror* or *Michelle Kwan: Heart of a Champion*. Then fill in the graphic organizer below with the most important ideas or events in the selection.

Selection: _____

Idea/ Event	Idea/ Event	Idea/ Event	Idea/ Event

Now write your summary of the selection on a separate sheet of paper. Remember to leave out details and minor events. Briefly restate the most important ideas or events in your own words.

Name _____

Paraphrasing

When you **paraphrase** a passage from a book, article, or story, you put it into your own words without changing the author's meaning. A careful writer makes sure to paraphrase without copying any passages word-for-word from the work of other writers.

Read the following passage from "La Bamba."

> But when Manuel did a fancy dance step, there was a burst of applause and some girls screamed. Manuel tried another dance step. He heard more applause and screams and started getting into the groove as he shivered and snaked around the stage. But the record got stuck, and he had to sing
>
> *Para bailar la bamba*
> *Para bailar la bamba*
> *Para bailar la bamba*
> *Para bailar la bamba*
> again and again.

Now read one fifth grader's paraphrase of the passage.

Paraphrase

> Manuel did one fancy dance step and then another. The audience applauded and screamed when he shivered and snaked across the stage. Then the record got stuck, and he sang one line of "La Bamba" again and again.

Improve the student's paraphrase by reducing it to a single sentence that tells what happened in the passage. You may want to reorder the information and reduce the number of details. Be sure to avoid repetition of whole phrases that appeared in the original passage. Write your improved version on the lines below.

_____

_____

Name _____

Have No Fear

Read the words in the chart. Then look in the word box to find a synonym and an antonym for each, and write these in the chart. Use a dictionary if you need help.

monotony
stationary
reckless
pain
disregard
strength
unafraid
uncertain
comfort
bewildered
mobile
untroubled
careful
focus
weakness
agitation
sure
frightened

	synonym	antonym
terrified		
dismayed		
excitement		
stamina		
concentrate		
discomfort		
unsure		
cautious		
immobile		

Choose a word from the word box and write your own sentence.

_____

_____

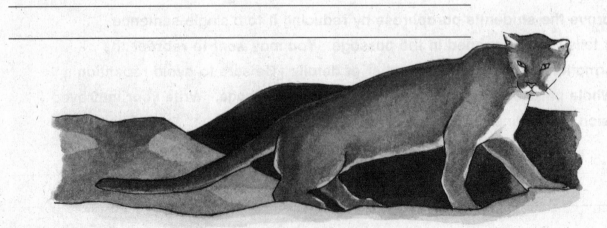

Name _____

I Predict . . .

Fill in the chart with your predictions, based on details from the selection and on what you know from personal experience.

Predicting Outcomes
selection details + personal knowledge + THINKING = prediction

Selection Details	Personal Knowledge
► Doug needs to get past a narrow ledge. ► The journey seems futile. ► Doug has made it to the narrow ledge before.	► People who have done something before, even if it was difficult, know that they can do it again.

Prediction: Doug will make it back to the ledge.

Selection Details	Personal Knowledge
_____ _____	_____ _____

Prediction: _____
_____

Selection Details	Personal Knowledge
_____ _____	_____ _____

Prediction: _____
_____

Name _____

Events Leading to the Climax

The events in *The Fear Place* lead to a climax when Doug must face his fear. Fill in the event map with sentences that describe the events that lead up to and come after the climax. Start at the bottom of the page.

7. Doug knows he is past the "fear place" when _____
_____

↑

6. When Doug reaches the narrowest part of the ledge, he _____
_____

↑

5. Doug reaches the "fear place" and _____

↑

4. Doug watches where Charlie goes and _____
_____

↑

3. Charlie _____

↑

2. Doug reaches the first ridge. He _____
_____

↑

1. Doug begins to climb, but _____

Name _____

Looking Forward

Read the passage. Then complete the activity on page 134.

The Apology

Alexa hadn't meant to break the bowl. In fact, she'd always loved that china bowl and its pretty blue pattern. But she had broken it, and all week she'd listened with dread for the phone call she knew would come. It would be Mrs. Holabird, their neighbor, calling to tell her mother about the accident.

The Holabirds had no children of their own, so they were especially fond of Alexa. She had been helping Mrs. Holabird with chores for about two years. When they went out of town, the Holabirds always paid Alexa to cat-sit for Misty. Alexa would come twice a day and refill Misty's food and water bowls. She usually stayed for a while, holding the big, silky cat on her lap and scratching her behind the ears. Sometimes she helped Misty exercise. It was fun to toss a ball or a catnip mouse into the air and watch the fat, fluffy cat leap and grab for it with her paws. How was she to know that Misty would crash into the bowl and knock it off its stand?

Alexa had been so horrified that she had hidden the broken pieces under the sideboard. She went home and fearfully awaited the phone call. But three days later it still had not come, even though the Holabirds had returned two days ago.

On the fourth morning, Alexa awoke with her mind made up. She put on her coat and walked to the front door, calling, "Mom, I need to go see Mr. and Mrs. Holabird."

Name _____

Looking Forward continued

Answer these questions about the passage on page 133.

1. What do you think Alexa will do next?

   _____

   _____

2. What clues in the passage helped you make this prediction?

   _____

   _____

   _____

3. Do you think Alexa's mother will be glad that Alexa apologized to

   Mrs. Holabird? Why or why not?

   _____

   _____

4. Do you think the Holabirds will ask Alexa to care for Misty again?
   Why or why not?

   _____

   _____

5. What might Alexa do to make up for breaking the bowl?

   _____

   _____

6. What is one thing Alexa might do differently the next time she plays
   with Misty?

   _____

   _____

Name _____

Nervous? No, Onward!

**Read this diary page. Underline each word with the suffix *-ward*
or *-ous*.**

The Hike

Climbing to the mountaintop was a frightening experience.
At first, it didn't seem so bad. The path upward was wide, even
spacious. After a while, though, I began to be nervous. The rise
was continuous, and the path began to narrow. When I looked
over the edge, I saw a monstrous gap between me and the canyon
bottom far below. Still, I made my way toward the top, pausing
only now and then. I knew that if I glanced backward, I would be
in trouble. Instead, I gazed outward to the golden plain in the
distance. It was a marvelous sight. I knew I would head homeward
in less than an hour.

Now write each word you underlined next to its meaning.

1. _____ : in a direction nearer
2. _____ : uncomfortable
3. _____ : in a direction away from
4. _____ : huge
5. _____ : toward where one lives
6. _____ : heading above
7. _____ : to the rear
8. _____ : roomy
9. _____ : ongoing, with no break
10. _____ : wonderful

Name _____

The /ôr/, /âr/, and /är/ Sounds

When you hear the /ôr/ sound, think of the patterns *or, oar,* and *ore.* When you hear the /âr/ sound, think of the patterns *are* and *air.* When you hear the /är/ sound, think of the pattern *ar.*

> /ôr/ t**or**ch, s**oar**, s**ore**   /âr/ h**are**, fl**air**   /är/ sc**ar**

► The vowel sound + *r* spellings of the starred words differ from the usual spelling patterns. The /ôr/ sound is spelled *ar* in *warn* and *oor* in *floor.*

Write each Spelling Word under its vowel + *r* sound.

/ôr/ Sound

_____

_____

_____

_____

_____

_____

_____

/âr/ Sound

_____

_____

_____

_____

_____

/är/ Sound

_____

_____

_____

Spelling Words
1. hare
2. scar
3. torch
4. soar
5. harsh
6. sore
7. lord
8. flair
9. warn*
10. floor*
11. tore
12. lair
13. snare
14. carve
15. bore
16. fare
17. gorge
18. barge
19. flare
20. rare

Name _____

Spelling Spree

Word Hunt Write the Spelling Word that you find in each of the longer words below.

Example: snowboarder *board*

1. torchlight _____
2. harebrained _____
3. warlord _____
4. scarcely _____
5. welfare _____
6. restored _____
7. floorshow _____

Alphabet Puzzler Write the Spelling Word that fits alphabetically between the two words in each group.

8. apple, _____, bicycle
9. butter, _____, dinner
10. ladder, _____, loan
11. sock, _____, stomach
12. father, _____, flame
13. harmful, _____, kitchen
14. sneeze, _____, solid
15. secret, _____, snow

Spelling Words

1. hare
2. scar
3. torch
4. soar
5. harsh
6. sore
7. lord
8. flair
9. warn*
10. floor*
11. tore
12. lair
13. snare
14. carve
15. bore
16. fare
17. gorge
18. barge
19. flare
20. rare

Proofreading and Writing

Proofreading Circle the five misspelled Spelling Words in this part of a note. Then write each word correctly.

To the Park Rangers:

    I have to leave unexpectedly for a day. Will you keep an eye on my two boys, who are camping on the north ledge? They are experienced climbers, but their tempers sometimes flar when they're alone with each other. For that matter, it's rair for them to get along anytime! The younger one has a sore knee from sliding down a gorg. I won't boar you with the details, but I would appreciate it if you could check on them during the day. I'll woarn them to behave themselves.

1. _____

2. _____

3. _____

4. _____

5. _____

Spelling Words

1. hare
2. scar
3. torch
4. soar
5. harsh
6. sore
7. lord
8. flair
9. warn*
10. floor*
11. tore
12. lair
13. snare
14. carve
15. bore
16. fare
17. gorge
18. barge
19. flare
20. rare

✏️ **Write a Prediction** Now that Doug has made it past the Fear Place, what do you think will happen next? Will he find his brother safe or in danger? Will Charlie continue to help him?

On a separate piece of paper, write a paragraph giving your prediction of what will happen next in the story. Use Spelling Words from the list.

Homophone Echoes

Match the letter of the correct definition to the underlined word. Then write the homophone pairs at the bottom of the page.

1. The hiker makes her way <u>through</u> a narrow canyon. _____

2. As she climbs, objects below <u>seem</u> to get smaller _____

3. She kneels beside the <u>burrow</u> of a ground squirrel. _____

4. In the distance she can see a snow-capped <u>peak</u>. _____

5. Will she <u>freeze</u> when she gets to the top? _____

6. She takes a quick <u>peek</u> into the canyon. _____

7. The <u>seam</u> in her boot rubs her heel. _____

8. She's a long way from the <u>borough</u> of Brooklyn! _____

9. If she <u>threw</u> a stone, it might cause a rockslide below. _____

10. Watching an eagle fly <u>frees</u> her from her fear. _____

a. in and out of
b. tossed
c. glance
d. stitch
e. appear
f. tunnel
g. liberates
h. summit
i. be cold
j. city section

11. _____ _____

12. _____ _____

13. _____ _____

14. _____ _____

15. _____ _____

Name _____

We Are Diving

Main Verbs and Helping Verbs A simple predicate can be more than one word. The **main verb** is the most important word in the predicate. The **helping verb** comes before the **main verb**.

    I **have climbed** the rope.   main verb: *climbed*   helping verb: *have*

Write the main verb and the helping verb in each of the following sentences.

1. This summer camp program has challenged me.

Main verb: _____

Helping verb: _____

2. I am facing my fear of water in the swimming classes.

Main verb: _____

Helping verb: _____

3. The swimming teacher has given me much encouragement.

Main verb: _____

Helping verb: _____

4. I have swum two laps so far this morning.

Main verb: _____

Helping verb: _____

5. Next summer, I will learn to dive!

Main verb: _____

Helping verb: _____

Name _____

Jellyfish Are Nasty

Linking Verbs A **linking verb** links the subject to a word in the predicate that names or describes the subject. It does not show action. A **predicate noun** following a linking verb names the subject. A **predicate adjective** following a linking verb describes the subject.

Common Linking Verbs

am	is	are	was	were	will be
look	feel	taste	smell	seem	appear

Underline the linking verb in each sentence below. Circle each predicate noun or predicate adjective. Write _PN_ on the line if the circled word is a predicate noun. Write _PA_ if it is a predicate adjective.

Example: I am a (swimmer.) PN

1. Susan will be a lifeguard someday. _____

2. Lifeguards are brave. _____

3. The ocean breeze smells fresh. _____

4. I am afraid of jellyfish. _____

5. A sea nettle is a jellyfish. _____

6. Ocean water tastes salty. _____

7. That boat is a kayak. _____

8. My grandmother was a diver. _____

9. That stroke seems difficult to me. _____

10. Clayton and Rachel are surfers. _____

Name _____

Are You Afraid?

Using Forms of the Verb *be* When using *be* as a linking verb, a writer must use the correct form of the verb. Like any other verb, a linking verb must agree with its subject in number.

	The Verb *be*	
	Present Tense	**Past Tense**
I	am	was
You	are	were
She/he/it	is	was
We	are	were
You	are	were
They	are	were

Identify the five incorrect forms of the verb *be* in the draft. Write the correct form of the verb above the error.

A long time ago, I were afraid of dogs. Every time I saw a dog I would stand absolutely still. Nobody could make me move until the dog were gone. I don't know why, but dogs was just frightening to me. My aunt said she would help me get to know her dog, Maggie. Maggie are a medium-sized dog. Every day for a month my aunt came to our house with Maggie. She were right. I began to trust Maggie and some other dogs too.

Name _____

Writing a Clarification Composition

Sometimes when you read, you will encounter a quote or statement that expresses a belief but whose meaning is not entirely clear. You can write a **clarification composition** to clarify the statement.

Choose one of the following statements and write it on the clarification map:

► *The only thing we have to fear is fear itself.*
    (Franklin D. Roosevelt)
► *Fools rush in where angels fear to tread.*
    (Alexander Pope)
► *Anything is possible, but not everything is probable.*
    (Doug Grillo)

Then write what you think the statement means, and list reasons, details, and examples from *The Fear Place* that support your opinion.

Statement
Meaning
Reasons, Details, and Examples

On a separate sheet of paper, write a three- to five-paragraph composition restating the statement in your own words and clarifying its meaning. Use examples from *The Fear Place* that support your opinion.

Name _____

Combining Sentences with Helping Verbs

Good writers avoid unnecessary repetition in their writing.
Sometimes you can improve your writing by combining
sentences that repeat the same helping verb into one sentence.

> He **had** reached the ledge. He **had** glanced down
> at the canyon.
> He **had** reached the ledge and glanced down at the
> canyon.

**Revise a postcard that Doug Grillo might have sent. Combine sentences that
repeat the same helping verb into a single sentence. Write the revised message
on the lines below.**

Dear Jim,

*We are finishing up our vacation in Colorado. We are coming home next week. I have
spotted a snowshoe rabbit. I have studied other wildlife for my merit badge. After a
fight, Gordie had hiked up a steep trail. My brother had pitched a tent on a high ridge.
I was very scared. I was determined to find my brother. I should have climbed with
someone else. I should have turned back before the narrow path curves sharply. Instead, I
faced my fear. With the help of Charlie the cougar, I reached my brother safely!*

Your friend,

Doug

_____

_____

_____

_____

_____

Name _____

Space Is the Place

Write each word from the box on the correct line.

Vocabulary

artificial

satellite

launches (*verb*)

orbit

reusable

mission

specialist

space shuttle

astronaut

weightlessness

1. spacecraft

_____

_____

2. people

_____

_____

3. descriptive words

_____

_____

4. words about movement

_____

_____

5. a condition

_____

Now choose three words from the box. Use them to write a short paragraph about the launch of a spacecraft.

_____

_____

_____

_____

_____

_____

Name _____

Main Idea Chart

Topic: _____	
Page 211	On September 12, 1992, Mae Jemison became the first African American woman to fly into space.
Pages 212–213	_____ _____
Pages 213–214	_____ _____
Pages 215–216	_____ _____
Page 217	_____ _____
Page 218	_____ _____
Pages 219–221	_____ _____
Pages 221–222	_____ _____

Name _____

Is It True?

The sentences below tell about Mae Jemison. Write T if the sentence is true, or F if the sentence is false. If a sentence is false, tell why it is false.

1. Mae Jemison developed an interest in science at an early age.

_____

_____

2. Her parents and teachers all encouraged her to become a scientist.

_____

_____

3. When she graduated from Stanford University, she applied for admission to the astronaut corps.

_____

_____

4. Mae never gave up her childhood dream of traveling in space.

_____

_____

5. At the end of her year of intensive training, Mae Jemison rode a rocket into space.

_____

_____

6. On September 12, 1992, Mae Jemison became the first African American woman to journey into space.

_____

_____

Name _____

Exploring the Topic

Read the following passage. Then complete the activity on page 149.

Space Shuttle Science

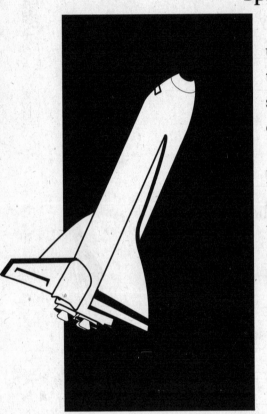

The space shuttle has many important uses. One use is for scientific research. In the weightless environment of space, scientists can carry out experiments they cannot do on Earth.

Inside the shuttle is a complete research laboratory called Spacelab. Spacelab is divided into two parts. One part is inside, where scientists can work. The other is outside and holds telescopes and other instruments that need to be exposed to space.

Most experiments take place in the inner section. Scientists on the space shuttle typically do experiments that make use of microgravity and weightlessness. They make new materials, such as crystals and silicon chips, and they also create medicines. Scientists even use themselves as test subjects, recording how weightlessness affects the human body.

Experiments in the outside section of Spacelab take advantage of being outside Earth's atmosphere. The atmosphere helps prevent radiation from reaching Earth, but it also makes radiation hard to study. Being outside the atmosphere also lets scientists use telescopes to get a clearer "view" of space.

Name _____

Exploring the Topic continued

Complete the chart below by filling in the topic and main ideas of the
passage on page 148. Then write two details that support one of the
main ideas.

Topic: _____

Main Ideas:	
first paragraph	1. _____
	_____
second paragraph	2. _____
	_____
third paragraph	3. _____
	_____
fourth paragraph	4. _____
	_____

Details:

1. _____

2. _____

Name _____

Suffix Shuttle

Choose words from the word boxes to write in the blanks in the paragraph below. Use the clue in parentheses to help you.

-ic	*-ive*
artistic	inventive
historic	massive
periodic	positive
realistic	supportive

It was a truly (timely) _____ event when the shuttle first went up. The scientists who built it had (clever) _____ ideas. They were dreamers, but they were (aware of how things are) _____ about what was possible. They knew the shuttle's flights would have to be (now and then) _____ during the year. But watching the (big) _____ rocket rise into the air was breathtaking. Its fiery trail in the sky looked (made with style) _____. The entire country was (in favor) _____ of their efforts. They were (sure) _____ they had a winner!

Name _____

The /ûr/ and /îr/ Sounds

When you hear the /ûr/ sound, think of the patterns *er, ir, ur, ear,* and *or.* When you hear the /îr/ sounds, think of the patterns *eer* and *ear:*

/ûr/ g**er**m, st**ir**, ret**ur**n, **ear**ly, w**or**th

/îr/ st**eer**, sm**ear**

► The /îr/ sound in *pier* differs from the usual spelling patterns. In this word it is spelled *ier:*

Write each Spelling Word under its vowel + *r* sound.

/ûr/ Sound

_____   _____
_____   _____
_____   _____
_____   _____
_____   _____
_____   _____
_____

/îr/ Sound

_____   _____

_____

Spelling Words

1. smear
2. germ
3. return
4. peer
5. stir
6. squirm
7. nerve
8. early
9. worth
10. pier*
11. thirst
12. burnt
13. rear
14. term
15. steer
16. pearl
17. squirt
18. perch
19. hurl
20. worse

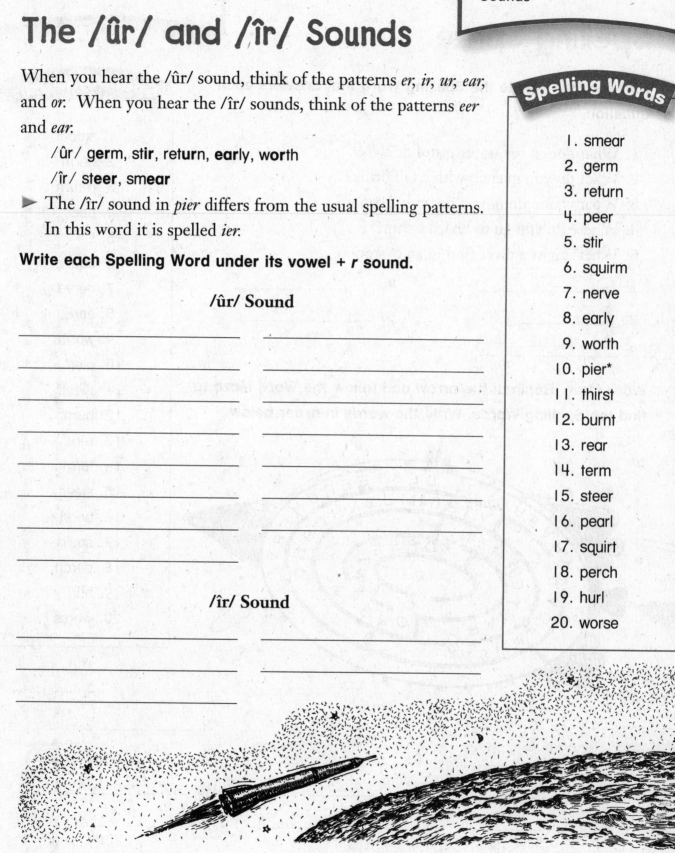

Name _____

Spelling Spree

Hint and Hunt Write the Spelling Word that answers each question.

1. What does a toy water pistol do?
2. What do you quench with a tall drink?
3. What is one thing you do with a spoon?
4. Where do you go to board a ship?
5. What might a diver find in an oyster?

1. _____   4. _____

2. _____   5. _____

3. _____

Word Maze Begin at the arrow and follow the Word Maze to find ten Spelling Words. Write the words in order below.

6. _____   9. _____   12. _____

7. _____   10. _____   13. _____

8. _____   11. _____   14. _____

                                           15. _____

Spelling Words

1. smear
2. germ
3. return
4. peer
5. stir
6. squirm
7. nerve
8. early
9. worth
10. pier*
11. thirst
12. burnt
13. rear
14. term
15. steer
16. pearl
17. squirt
18. perch
19. hurl
20. worse

Proofreading and Writing

Proofreading Circle the five misspelled Spelling Words in this part of a script for a class skit. Then write each word correctly.

Astronaut:	Mission Control, when can we begin our retern to Earth?
Mission Control:	Probably erly tomorrow morning. How's it going up there? How much fuel have you burnt?
Astronaut:	Not much—we've still got a few days' werth. We're all starting to squerm a bit up here, though. We're ready to go home. Actually, if I per closely through the glass here, I think I can see my house.
Mission Control:	That's very funny.

1. _____

2. _____

3. _____

4. _____

5. _____

Spelling Words

1. smear
2. germ
3. return
4. peer
5. stir
6. squirm
7. nerve
8. early
9. worth
10. pier*
11. thirst
12. burnt
13. rear
14. term
15. steer
16. pearl
17. squirt
18. perch
19. hurl
20. worse

✏️ **Write a Newspaper Article** You have been asked to write a brief article about Mae Jemison's space shuttle mission for the school newspaper. Did any one of the experiments particularly interest you? Will you include any details about Jemison's personal life?

On a separate piece of paper, write your article about Mae Jemison's mission. Use Spelling Words from the list.

Stress on Syllables

Read each dictionary entry. Sound out the entry word three ways, placing stress on a different syllable each time. Circle the choice with the correct stress.

1. ad/ven/ture (ăd vĕn chər) *n.* A bold, dangerous, or risky undertaking.
   AD/ven/ture   ad/VEN/ture   ad/ven/TURE

2. en/gi/neer/ing (ĕn jə nîr ing) *n.* The practical use of scientific knowledge.
   EN/gi/neer/ing   en/GI/neer/ing   en/gi/NEER/ing

3. en/vi/ron/ment (ĕn vī rən mənt) *n.* Surroundings and conditions that affect the growth of living things.
   en/VI/ron/ment   en/vi/RON/ment   en/vi/ron/MENT

4. in/flu/ence (ĭn flōō əns) *n.* The power to have an effect without using direct force.
   IN/flu/ence   in/FLU/ence   in/flu/ENCE

5. or/gan/i/za/tion (ôr gən ĭ zā shən) *n.* A group of people united for some purpose or work.
   OR/gan/i/za/tion   or/GAN/i/za/tion   or/gan/i/ZA/tion

6. par/tic/i/pate (pär tĭs ə pāt) *v.* To join with others in doing something; take part.
   par/TIC/i/pate   par/tic/I/pate   par/tic/i/PATE

7. tel/e/vi/sion (tĕl ə vĭ zhən) *n.* The transmission and reception of visual images and sounds as electrical waves through the air or through wires.
   TEL/e/vi/sion   tel/e/VI/sion   tel/e/vi/SION

8. vol/un/teer (vŏl ən tîr) *n.* A person who performs a service of his or her own free will.
   VOL/un/teer   vol/UN/teer   vol/un/TEER

Astronauts Travel into Space

Verb Tenses Verbs have forms, or tenses, that tell when the action
occurs.

► A **present-tense** verb shows action that happens now,
  or that happens regularly over time.

► A **past-tense** verb shows that something already occurred.

► To form the **present tense,** add *-s* or *-es* to most verbs
  if the subject is singular. Do not add *-s* or *-es* if the subject
  is plural or *I* or *you*.

► To form the **past tense** of most verbs, add *-ed*.

**On the line, write the tense of the verb in the first sentence
of each pair. Then fill in the blank of the second sentence with
the same verb, but change its tense.**

Example: Astronauts conducted experiments in space. ____past____

Astronauts __conduct__ experiments in space.

1. My mother studies engineering at the university. _____

   My mother _____ engineering at the university.

2. You learned about space travel in school. _____

   You _____ about space travel in school.

3. I worked hard on my science project. _____

   I _____ hard on my science project.

4. Kate's father designs bridges. _____

   Kate's father _____ bridges.

5. She followed her dreams. _____

   She _____ her dreams.

Name _____

Astronauts Will Travel into Space

More about Verbs A **future-tense** verb shows that something is going to happen. Form the **future tense** by using the helping verb *will* or *shall* with the main verb.

Present Tense: I **see** many films about space.

Future Tense: I **will see** many films about space.

Present Tense: He **reads** about Jupiter.

Future Tense: He **shall read** about Jupiter.

Rewrite each sentence. Change each verb from the present or past tense to the future tense.

Example: You go to Cape Canaveral.

You will go to Cape Canaveral.

1. Astronauts fly the space shuttle.

_____

2. The space probe landed on Mars.

_____

3. You studied physics in college.

_____

4. Meteors shoot across the sky.

_____

5. We think about the future.

_____

Name _____

I Joined

Using the Right Tense A good writer uses the correct tense to talk about a particular time. Look at the two examples below. The second sentence in each pair makes more sense than the first sentence.

Incorrect: I will clean my room yesterday.
Correct: I cleaned my room yesterday.
Incorrect: Next Thursday Jeremy listens to me on the radio.
Correct: Next Thursday Jeremy will listen to me on the radio.

George has written a paragraph about his dream of joining the Peace Corps, like Mae Jemison and his teacher. Revise the paragraph to correct problems with verb tenses.

will go
Example: Next week, we went to South America.
                                              ^

Someday, I joined the Peace Corps. Last month, my teacher Mr.

Stinson talks about his experience as a member of the Peace Corps in

Ghana. He shows us photographs of the region too. He made many

new friends while he was there. In the Peace Corps, my teacher

will work to help build a school. Every day now I asked him to tell us

more about it.

Name _____

Writing a Business Letter

When Mae Jemison applied to the National Aeronautics and Space Administration to become an astronaut, she wrote a business letter. You write a **business letter** to apply for a job, to request or persuade someone to do something, to order a product from ads or catalogs, to ask for information, to complain about a product or service, or to express an opinion to a newspaper, or to a radio or TV station.

On a separate sheet of paper, plan and organize a business letter. Either write a letter of recommendation to NASA telling why Mae Jemison would make an excellent astronaut, or write to a company asking for information. Follow these steps:

1. Write a **heading** (your own address and the date) in the upper right corner.

2. Write the **inside address** (the address of the person or business you are writing to) at the left margin.

3. Write a **greeting** (*Dear Sir or Madam:* or *Dear [business name]:*) at the left margin below the inside address.

4. Write the **body** of your letter below the greeting. Be brief and direct, but present all of the necessary details clearly. If you state an opinion, support it with details. If you order a product, identify the item, size, color, price, and quantity you want. Make sure to use a formal and polite tone.

5. Write a formal **closing** such as *Sincerely, Cordially,* or *Yours truly* in the lower right corner.

6. Sign your full name under the closing. Then print or type your name below your **signature**.

When you finish planning your business letter, copy it onto a clean sheet of paper. Then share it with a classmate or send it to the company you wrote to.

Name _____

Using the Right Tone

Tone is the attitude that a writer has toward a subject and is conveyed in the choice of words and details. Here are some tips to follow when you write a business letter:

► Use polite language and a formal tone.

► Use correct grammar and complete sentences.

► Avoid the use of slang.

► Do not include personal information.

Fill in the chart with examples of language and details that do *not* strike the proper tone.

144 Primrose Street
Evanston, IL 60201
October 23, 2001

Dr. Mae Jemison
P.O. Box 591455
Houston, TX 77259-1455
Dear Mae,

    I am in the fifth grade at Primrose Elementary School. My class will be studying about space and space travel. I got a 91 on my last quiz. We hope you might be able to come talk to our class about your experiences as an astronaut.

    It would be the bomb to meet an astronaut in person. My uncle is a pilot. We look forward to hearing from you. Do not give us some lame excuse about why you cannot speak here.

            Love,
            Karen Aldrin

Slang:	
Impolite Language:	
Informal Tone:	
Personal Information:	

Name _____

Iditarod History

Use the words in the box to complete the article about the Iditarod Trail Race.

> ## Vocabulary
>
> obstacles   spectators   pace   musher   checkpoint   cargo

The Iditarod Trail Sled Dog Race celebrates one of the most famous events in Alaska's history. In 1925, a serious illness struck the city of Nome. The closest supply of medicine was far across the state in Anchorage. Twenty men drove their dog teams up the Iditarod Trail in a long relay. Each _____ drove his team at a fast _____ to bring the medicine to Nome. The precious _____ of medicine arrived in Nome only a week after it left Anchorage.

In the late 1960s, several Alaskans wanted to honor their state's 100th anniversary. They proposed a dog sled race along the Iditarod Trail. The U.S. Army helped clear the old trail of _____, and in 1973, the first modern Iditarod race was held.

Today, volunteers inspect and monitor the teams at over twenty _____ along the trail. Thousands of _____ line the racecourse to watch the competition.

Name _____

What Will Happen?

Fill in this Predicting Outcomes chart as you read the Paired Selections.

	Iditarod Dream	*Me, Mop, and the Moondance Kid*
Details about the main character	1. _____ _____ 2. _____ _____ 3. _____ _____	1. _____ _____ 2. _____ _____ 3. _____ _____
Details about the character's team	1. _____ _____ 2. _____ _____	1. _____ _____ 2. _____ _____
What will happen after the selection ends?	_____ _____ _____ _____	_____ _____ _____ _____

Name _____

Discuss Photographs

Use the chart below to compare and contrast the photographs in this theme.

Iditarod Dream

Photographs	What Is Shown	How the Photos Add to the Story
page 230C		
page 230G		
page 230I		

Michelle Kwan: Heart of a Champion

Photographs	What Is Shown	How the Photos Add to the Story
page 141		
page 142		
page 145		

Mae Jemison: Space Scientist

Photographs	What Is Shown	How the Photos Add to the Story
page 212		
page 214		
page 222		

Name _____

Fly Ball Words

Use the words from the box to complete the sentences below.

Vocabulary

inning	play-offs	backstop
foul	respectable	control

- When each team makes three outs, the _____ is over.

- The best pitchers have great _____. They can put the ball wherever they want.

- The catcher fields most _____ pop-ups between home plate and the _____.

- Only teams with a _____ number of wins make the league _____ at the end of the season.

Now use four of the vocabulary words in sentences of your own.

_____

_____

_____

_____

Name _____

Test Practice

Use the three steps you've learned to complete these sentences about _Me, Mop, and the Moondance Kid._ Fill in the circle for the best answer in the answer row at the bottom of the page.

1. _Me, Mop, and the Moondance Kid_ is told from the point of view of

    _____.

    A T.J.   **C** Moondance

    B Mop   **D** Dad

2. Dad is discouraged with the Elks because they _____.

    F do not take his advice   **H** do not have a good coach

    G do not show his sons respect **J** are not playing well

3. Moondance's pitching problem is that _____.

    A he gets nervous when others are watching

    B he is afraid of hitting someone with the ball

    C he does not throw the ball fast enough

    D he does not listen to advice from others

4. **Connecting/Comparing** Think about _Me, Mop, and the Moondance Kid_ and _Iditarod Dream._ T.J. and Dusty are alike in that both boys

    _____.

    F are overly confident about their abilities

    G blame their failures on others

    H make a mistake during a competition

    J feel they have disappointed their parents

ANSWER ROWS   **I**   Ⓐ Ⓑ Ⓒ Ⓓ   **3** Ⓐ Ⓑ Ⓒ Ⓓ

                 2 Ⓕ Ⓖ Ⓗ Ⓙ   **4** Ⓕ Ⓖ Ⓗ Ⓙ

Continue on page 166.

Test Practice continued

5. Dad asks Sister Carmelita to help Moondance because she

_____.

   A used to be a good pitcher   **C** is a Little League coach

   B played professional baseball   **D** likes to help others

6. Moondance probably feels that he _____.

   F can be a good pitcher without Titi's help

   G should play basketball instead

   H can become a professional baseball player

   J will never be good enough to please Dad

7. The author wrote *Me, Mop, and the Moondance Kid* in order to

_____.

   A tell a story about two sons and their father

   B persuade young people to play baseball

   C tell the story of a professional baseball player

   D describe how to pitch a baseball

8. **Connecting/Comparing** Both Moondance and Michelle Kwan

understand that _____.

   F coaches don't always give the best advice

   G parents can expect too much from children

   H improving your performance can be challenging

   J performing for an audience is fun

ANSWER ROWS 5 Ⓐ Ⓑ Ⓒ Ⓓ   7 Ⓐ Ⓑ Ⓒ Ⓓ

                 6 Ⓕ Ⓖ Ⓗ Ⓙ   8 Ⓕ Ⓖ Ⓗ Ⓙ

Name _____

Fact or Opinion?

Read each statement below. Write _F_ if the statement is a fact and _O_ if the statement is an opinion.

1. The Junior Iditarod is two days long. _____

2. It is the hardest sled dog race in all of Alaska. _____

3. The race winds along a trail in the forest. _____

4. Sled dogs are small but very strong. _____

5. I believe snowmobiles should stay off the race course. _____

6. A musher's worst nightmare is running into a moose. _____

7. Sled drivers sometimes run alongside their sleds. _____

8. When racers reach the halfway point, they must stay with their dogs.

   _____

9. The most difficult part of the race is near the finish line. _____

10. You must win the race to have fun. _____

Name _____

What's It All About?

Read the passage below. Then complete the chart by filling in the topic and main ideas. Also add two details from the passage that support each main idea.

The Iditarod Trail Sled Dog Race takes place each winter in Alaska. It is run on a 1,150-mile trail from Anchorage to Nome. Mushers and dog teams cover the distance in about 10 to 17 days. They cross frozen rivers and lakes. They make their way through dense forests and past jagged mountains. The temperature is often well below zero degrees Fahrenheit.

The first Iditarod Trail Race took place in 1973. All twenty-two mushers were men. Almost all were from Alaska. The very next year women joined the race, and Mary Shields became the first woman to finish, placing 23rd. In 1985, Libby Riddles became the first woman to win the Iditarod. Since its beginnings, the race has welcomed mushers from more than 20 states and 13 nations, including Japan, Australia, and Czechoslovakia. In 2003, the winner was Robert Sørlie, a firefighter from Norway, who became the second non-Alaskan to win the race.

Topic: _____

Main Idea: _____

Details: _____

_____

_____

Main Idea: _____

Details: _____

_____

_____

Name _____

Find the Suffix

Read the sentences. Underline the word in each sentence with the suffix -*ous* or the suffix -*ward*. Then write the meaning of the word.

1. My uncle told me a humorous story from his youth.

   _____

2. The story began on a train moving westward from Denver.

   _____

3. The train soon entered mountainous country.

   _____

4. The train made a continuous *clickity-clack* as it passed over the rails.

   _____

5. Suddenly the train came to a stop and began moving backward.

   _____

6. My uncle glanced anxiously at the other passengers.

   _____

7. A little later the train started moving forward again.

   _____

8. The conductor entered the car with a tremendous smile on his face.

   _____

9. The engineer had seen a poisonous snake on the tracks and was

   backing away from it. _____

10. "That was simply ridiculous," my uncle said. "He could have scared

    it with the whistle." _____

Name _____

Write the Right Word!

Read the homophone pairs and the sentence next to them. Use context to help you figure out which word to write in each blank.

1. ant/aunt   My _____ found an
_____ in her kitchen.

2. read/red   We _____ about
_____ and white blood cells for science class.

3. close/clothes   _____ the dryer before all the
_____ tumble out!

4. hall/haul   You'll have to _____ your suitcase to your
room down the _____.

5. soar/sore   Even with a _____ wing, the hawk could
_____ high overhead.

6. tide/tied   The girls _____ up the boat so it wouldn't
drift out on the _____.

7. blew/blue   Jacqueline _____ the
_____ candle out.

8. knew/new   Wes _____ the school had a
_____ gymnasium.

9. their/there   How many students left _____ jackets
_____?

10. wait/weight   Dana's little brother couldn't _____
until his _____ reached 40 pounds.

Name _____

Spelling Review

Write Spelling Words from the list on this page to answer the questions.

1–8. Which eight words have the /ou/, /ô/, or /oi/ sounds?

1. _____ 5. _____

2. _____ 6. _____

3. _____ 7. _____

4. _____ 8. _____

9–26. Which eighteen words have the /ôr/, /âr/, /är/, /ûr/, or /îr/ sounds?

9. _____ 18. _____

10. _____ 19. _____

11. _____ 20. _____

12. _____ 21. _____

13. _____ 22. _____

14. _____ 23. _____

15. _____ 24. _____

16. _____ 25. _____

17. _____ 26. _____

27–30. Which four compound words have one of these words in them?

end   wild   test   date

27. _____ 29. _____

28. _____ 30. _____

Spelling Words

1. halt
2. weekend
3. steer
4. gorge
5. first aid
6. smear
7. thousand
8. wildlife
9. hurl
10. brother-in-law
11. perch
12. test tube
13. wheelchair
14. early
15. noisy
16. launch
17. hawk
18. royal
19. worth
20. soar
21. pearl
22. up-to-date
23. tore
24. stir
25. snare
26. flair
27. carve
28. barge
29. coward
30. return

Theme 2: **Give It All You've Got**   171

Name _____

Spelling Spree

Rhyme Time Write a Spelling Word that rhymes with the underlined word and makes sense in the sentence.

1. Marge, do you see that <u>large</u> _____?

2. <u>Howard</u>, how did you spell the word _____?

3. If the plane will _____, we will <u>roar</u>.

4. Let us <u>forge</u> ahead through the narrow _____.

5. I <u>wore</u> my new shirt until it _____.

6. Please _____ the ball to the girl with the <u>curl</u>.

7. Nate, please <u>rate</u> our new _____ <u>gate</u>.

The Third Word Write the Spelling Word that belongs in each group.

8. to come back, to revisit, to _____

9. diamond, ruby, _____

10. sister-in-law, father-in-law, _____

11. to balance, to wobble, to _____

12. ten, hundred, _____

13. days off, holiday, _____

14. to start, to begin, to _____

15. animals, nature, _____

Spelling Words

1. weekend
2. coward
3. soar
4. up-to-date
5. brother-in-law
6. gorge
7. tore
8. thousand
9. wildlife
10. barge
11. launch
12. return
13. perch
14. pearl
15. hurl

Name _____

Proofreading and Writing

Proofreading Circle the six misspelled Spelling Words in this diary entry. Then write each word correctly.

April 18—This weekend I woke up erly to go to the race. At the track, I passed the first ade station and steered my weelchair into place at the starting line. The crowd was noysy. I didn't win, but I felt like a royel princess when I came to a hault at the finish line.

1. _____   4. _____

2. _____   5. _____

3. _____   6. _____

Spelling Words

1. halt
2. noisy
3. early
4. hawk
5. test tube
6. snare
7. wheelchair
8. flair
9. steer
10. carve
11. stir
12. worth
13. smear
14. royal
15. first aid

Revise a Letter Write Spelling Words to complete the letter.

You should have seen me _____ through the pack during the race! I flew like a _____. Then I felt like I was caught in a _____ when I hit some loose gravel. I recovered quickly. Racing is hard, but it is _____ the effort. I have a real _____ for it, I think.

School was fun today. For art class, I started to _____ a horse out of soap. Then in science I had to _____ a solution and put it in a _____. Last, we had to _____ pond water on a slide and look at it under a microscope.

✏️ **Write an Article** On a separate sheet of paper, write a short newspaper article about a race or sport you enjoy. Use the Spelling Review Words.

Name _____

Working with Common, Proper, and Possessive Nouns

Copy the nouns from the following sentences into the appropriate columns below. When you rewrite a proper noun, be sure to capitalize correctly.

1. Dusty has many good dogs.
2. This young musher heads for the Iditarod Trail.
3. The team must pull the sled safely back to Wasilla.
4. The snow is usually deep in January and February.

Common Nouns	**Proper Nouns**
_____	_____
_____	_____
_____	_____
_____	_____

Complete each sentence by writing the possessive form of the noun shown in parentheses. Circle each plural possessive noun you write.

5. The _____ feet are cold. (musher)

6. The _____ coats are thick. (dogs)

7. The _____ faces are red. (handlers)

8. The _____ runners are icy. (sled)

9. The _____ smile shows his happiness. (winner)

Name _____

Identifying Action Verbs and Direct Objects

Underline each action verb. Circle each direct object. Not every sentence has a direct object.

1. The pitcher throws the ball.

2. The batter swings hard.

3. She hits a long fly.

4. The right fielder raises his glove.

5. The ball flies over the glove.

6. The ball bounces to the fence.

7. The right fielder grabs the ball.

8. He fires a bullet to the third baseman.

9. The third baseman tags the runner.

10. The runner touched the base before the tag.

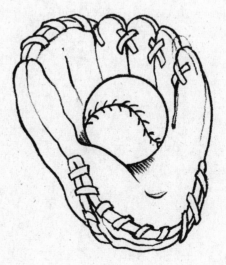

Name _____

Poetry Pen Pals

Use words from the box to complete the letter below.

January 21, 2002

Dear Amy,

Hi! How are you? I am starting to enjoy my new home in
Pennsylvania, but I still miss Hillside Elementary very much. I
also miss the warm weather! I have been writing a lot since
we moved. I am sending you a _____ to read that I
wrote a few months ago. I tried to make the last word in
each line _____, but sometimes the words were
too unusual. The poem is about taking a walk in the winter,
and I tried to create the _____ and sound of feet
walking in crunchy snow. My favorite _____ is of
the snow swirling around the streetlights. I would love to
hear what you think about it. I found out that writing poetry
takes a lot of creativity and _____! Please let me
know if you like it. I miss you!

Your friend,

Wendy

**Write a short reply from Amy to Wendy, using each of the vocabulary
words at least once.**

_____

_____

_____

_____

_____

Vocabulary

poem

rhythm

rhyme

imagination

image

Name _____

Elements of Poetry

Look for these elements in the poems

Places and Seasons: List words that show sensory details.

Poem _____	Poem _____

Animals: List rhyme patterns and repetition.

Poem _____	Poem _____

People: List words that describe the mood.

Poem _____	Poem _____

Name _____

Two Poems

Choose two poems: one that rhymes and follows a pattern, and one that doesn't, called free verse. On the chart below, compare the two poems by answering the questions.

	Rhyming Poem _____ Title	**Free Verse Poem** _____ Title
What is the poem about?		
What word or sound patterns are in the poem?		
What word pictures does the poem create?		

Name _____

Poetry Award

You are the poetry editor for a magazine. Choose one poem from
Focus on Poetry **as the Poem of the Year. Tell what makes it a**
good poem and why people will want to read it.

Poem of the Year

_____

I think this poem is the best because

_____

_____

_____

_____

_____

_____

_____

_____

_____

_____

_____

_____

_____

_____

_____

Name _____

Analyzing a Poem

Choose another poem to study closely. Make notes about sensory words, rhyme, repetition, and mood on the chart. Then write a paragraph that describes how the poem uses each of these elements. Use examples to support your ideas.

Poem: _____

Sensory Words	
Rhyme	
Repetition	
Mood	

_____

_____

_____

_____

_____

Poetic Dreams

**Read this diary entry. In the underlined words, circle the suffixes
-*ward*, -*ous*, -*ive*, and *ic*.**

Dear Diary,

We wrote poems in class today. The teacher told us to think of a <u>joyous</u> or
memorable experience from our lives. She reminded us to use <u>active</u>, lively
language with vivid images. I was leaning <u>toward</u> writing about the
<u>wondrous</u> landscape I saw during my trip to the mountains. The teacher
called out <u>instructive</u> hints as we wrote, but I was still having trouble getting
started. I decided to read the work of some <u>historic</u> poets for inspiration. I
read a few poems by Robert Frost and Emily Dickinson, and then I was
excited to start my own. I wrote about the long, <u>continuous</u> path we hiked
in the mountains. I described the <u>marvelous</u> views and the sense of peace
I felt as we hiked <u>downward</u>. When I finished the poem, I was very happy
with it. Maybe someday I will be a <u>famous</u> poet!

**Now, write each underlined word from the
diary entry beside its correct definition.**

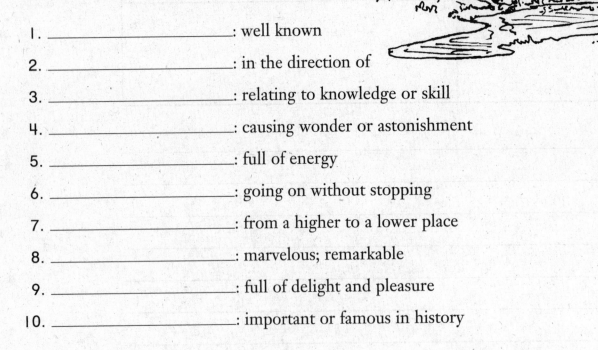

1. _____ : well known

2. _____ : in the direction of

3. _____ : relating to knowledge or skill

4. _____ : causing wonder or astonishment

5. _____ : full of energy

6. _____ : going on without stopping

7. _____ : from a higher to a lower place

8. _____ : marvelous; remarkable

9. _____ : full of delight and pleasure

10. _____ : important or famous in history

Name _____

Homophones

Remember that homophones are words that sound alike but have different spellings and meanings.

/pān/ **pain** "physical suffering caused by injury"

/pān/ **pane** "a sheet of glass"

Write each pair of Spelling Words under the heading that names their vowel sound.

Spelling Words

1. cord
2. chord
3. pray
4. prey
5. seam
6. seem
7. sole
8. soul
9. piece
10. peace
11. role
12. roll
13. peel
14. peal
15. shone
16. shown
17. pain
18. pane
19. pole
20. poll

/ā/ Sound

/ē/ Sound

/ō/ Sound

/ôr/ Sounds

Name _____

Spelling Spree

Book Titles Write the Spelling Word that correctly completes each book title. Remember to use capital letters.

1. _____ Over! 50 Dog Tricks by K. Nyne

2. How Lions Hunt for _____ by Tawny Katz

3. The Torn _____: A Guide for Tailors by So Ng

4. Love, _____, and Happiness by Flow R. Child

5. My Starring _____ in Movies by I. M. Cool

6. How to Fix the _____ of a Shoe by Cobb Lurr

7. Using Every Potato _____: Learning to
   Compost by Rich Soyl

8. The Sun _____ Down by Clair Skye

9. The Broken _____ of Glass by Ike N. Ficksitt

10. Play That _____: A Beginner's Guide to the
    Guitar by Ivana Strumm

Hidden Words Write the Spelling Word that is hidden in each row of letters. Don't let the other words fool you!

11. leapollocal _____

12. francorder _____

13. classoulilby _____

14. blimprayellow _____

15. blesseempire _____

16. trapoless _____

17. cashownersh _____

18. propaincons _____

19. capiecertay _____

20. appealisie _____

Name _____

Proofreading and Writing

Proofreading Circle the five misspelled Spelling Words in this poem. Then write each word correctly.

Lighten Up

Through the paine of dirty glass,
Dark clouds glowered.
I felt listless, sad, grumpy.
Then, with the energy of a small child,
A seme of sunlight shoon through the clouds,
Bursting through the gloom.
That sole peice of light
Wakened my sol, calling,
"Lighten up!"

1. _____
2. _____
3. _____
4. _____
5. _____

Copyright © Houghton Mifflin Company. All rights reserved.

Spelling Words

1. cord
2. chord
3. pray
4. prey
5. seam
6. seem
7. sole
8. soul
9. piece
10. peace
11. role
12. roll
13. peel
14. peal
15. shone
16. shown
17. pain
18. pane
19. pole
20. poll

✎ **Write a Song** The words to many songs are often very poetic. The songwriter may express feelings or send a message to listeners. Think of a topic that you would like to write a song about, and think of a favorite tune.

On a separate sheet of paper, write new song lyrics to go with a familiar tune. Use Spelling Words from the list.

Name _____

Borrowed Language

Read each entry word, its origin, and its definition on the dictionary page below. Then fill in the correct word in each sentence below.

> **caveat** (Latin): a warning or explanation
>
> **cuisine** (French): a particular type of cooking
>
> **encore** (French): an additional performance
>
> **habitat** (Latin): the place or environment where a person or thing is most likely to live
>
> **memento** (Latin): something that serves as a reminder
>
> **modus operandi** (Latin): a way of operating or functioning
>
> **pronto** (Spanish): without delay; quickly
>
> **siesta** (Spanish): a nap

1. After thunderous applause from the audience, the singer reappeared

   on stage and agreed to do an _____.

2. She keeps an old pink slipper as a _____ of her

   dancing days.

3. Leo's unusual _____ makes no sense to his coworkers,

   who prefer not to do everything backward.

4. If we don't get moving _____, we won't get to the

   bake sale before the cookies are gone.

5. I have just one _____: if I can't have dessert, I won't

   eat my spinach.

6. I yawned and took a _____ during the opera star's

   performance.

7. My lizard, Eddie, prefers a dry, desert-like _____.

8. Eddie's favorite _____ is Chinese takeout, although

   he enjoys French food too.

Name _____

A Family of Poets

Capitalizing Nouns That Replace Names Use a capital letter with a
noun that replaces a name.

Write the correct word to complete each sentence.

1. My (mother, Mother) writes poetry. _____

2. She reads her poems to my (brother, Brother) and me.
   _____

3. Sometimes she asks (dad, Dad) what he thinks, too.
   _____

4. Mom knows that (grandma, Grandma) has a good ear for rhythm.
   _____

5. My little (sister, Sister) enjoys poems that rhyme.
   _____

6. Grandfather Richards, my mother's (father, Father), writes
   funny limericks. _____

7. Does your (grandfather, Grandfather) write limericks?
   _____

9. Sometimes (mom, Mom) wants me to help her

   choose the best word. _____

10. "Hey, (sis, Sis), please help me with this

   rhyme." _____

Name _____

Hoop Season

Keeping Verbs in the Same Tense Be careful not to change verb
tenses unnecessarily in the middle of a paragraph.

**Write the correct verb forms that complete the
sentence in this description of a basketball game.**

    Last night Dad and I (go, went) to a
basketball game. The fans (shout, shouted)
greetings to their favorite players, and some players
(waved, wave) back.

    When the buzzer (rings, rang), the players
(charged, will charge) onto the court. The game (is,
was) slow for the first quarter. At halftime, people
(will crowd, crowded) the aisles and (munched, will
munch) popcorn.

    In the second half, one guard suddenly
(passes, passed) the ball to the forward, who (pivots,
pivoted), (dribbled, will dribble) the ball, and
(ducked, will duck) under her opponent's
outstretched arms. She (hands, handed) the ball to
the center, who (slammed, slams) it through the
hoop. The fans (roar, roared)!

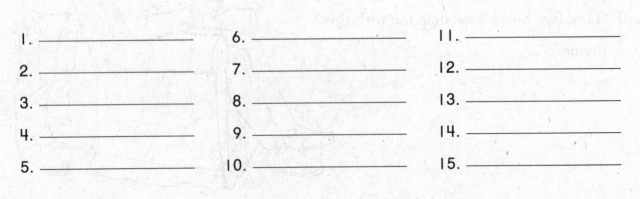

1. _____
2. _____
3. _____
4. _____
5. _____

6. _____
7. _____
8. _____
9. _____
10. _____

11. _____
12. _____
13. _____
14. _____
15. _____

Name _____

Family Reunion

Using Capital Letters Correctly Capitalize a noun that names a
particular person, place, or thing. Capitalize a word that takes the
place of a name.

**Use proofreading marks to correct the ten errors in punctuation
and capitalization in these observations for a poem.**

Example: every fall our Family has a reunion at harvest time!

Ten cars full of relatives turn at the Sign pointing to fox

hollow. Their cars bounce into grandmas' front yard and putter

to a stop.

Everyone helps with the cooking. Aunt Marylou washes and cuts

greens. One Cousin stirs batter for a huge pan of cornbread. The other

Aunts help my mother prepare the tables. In the back, all the uncles

gather around the barbecue and tease uncle Don. He and Dad always

take charge of cooking the chicken and the ribs.

Cousins chase each other through the cornfield on this

sunny october day. What a wonderful day we have?

Name _____

Planning a Poem

Put the most important ideas for your poem in the first column. If your poem tells a story, list the events. If your poem describes a person, place, thing, or memory, list its main features or actions. Then add details about each item and some of the exact words you'll use.

Topic: _____

The mood I want to express: _____

Main Events or Features	Descriptive Details

Exact Words (sense words, adjectives, and so on)	Rhyme Words

Name _____

Words That Sound Like What They Mean

Read each sentence. Choose the best word to complete it, and write it on the blank.

| grumble |
| sizzling |
| scuff |
| tickle |
| snap |
| rattle |
| fizzy |
| musty |
| stomp |
| fluttering |
| whiny |
| clap |
| squawk |
| slippery |
| crumple |
| shrill |
| slosh |
| shiver |

1. At the picnic I enjoy a hot _____ burger.

2. I drink fruit punch that is _____ and cold.

3. We _____ the paper plates after we eat.

4. The pots and pans _____ as we wash them.

5. Later I walk on the beach and _____ the sand.

6. I like the rhythm of the waves as they _____ on to shore.

7. As I wade along the shore, I feel water _____ my feet.

8. Above my head, the sea gulls _____ at one another.

9. I _____ my hands to make them fly away.

10. My sweatshirt keeps me warm so I don't _____.

Write two sentences of your own. Use a word that sounds like what it means in each sentence. Use words from the box, or choose your own.

11. _____

_____

_____

12. _____

_____

_____

Name _____

Voices of the Revolution

After reading each selection, complete the chart below and on the next page to show what you discovered.

	And Then What Happened, Paul Revere?	**Katie's Trunk**	**James Forten**
What kind of writing is this selection an example of?			
Why was this story important to tell?			
What character traits are revealed by the character's actions?			

Name _____

Voices of the Revolution continued

	And Then What Happened, Paul Revere?	Katie's Trunk	James Forten
What details about colonial life did you learn from the selection?			
What do you think the author's purpose for writing this selection was?			

How did the selections in *Voices of the Revolution* increase your understanding of life in that period?

_____

_____

_____

Name _____

Resisting Oppression

Use the words in the box to complete the paragraphs below.

The residents of America's thirteen _____

resented the new _____ levied on them by

the British government. A group of citizens in the Boston area

formed a secret club to _____ England's

method of governing America. The organization was known as

the Sons of Liberty, and every member was a

_____. The group won a place in history

when its members dumped a _____ of tea

into Boston Harbor to protest the tax on that commodity.

As it became clear that England would never allow the colonists

a voice in their own government, Americans began discussing the

possibility of _____. That kind of talk was

dangerous, though, so messages were carried secretly by

_____ riders from one city to another. The

riders had to elude _____ or they would be

deprived of their _____. The communications

network they established proved to be very valuable when war

finally broke out.

Choose one of the vocabulary words and write a sentence.

_____

_____

Vocabulary

revolution

express

cargo

colonies

oppose

liberty

Patriot

sentries

taxes

Name _____

Fact or Opinion?

**Fill in the chart with facts or opinions from the pages indicated
in the first column. Where indicated, explain why the viewpoint
is a fact or an opinion.**

Page	Statement	Fact or Opinion	Viewpoint Revealed
263	"Of all the busy people in Boston, Paul Revere would turn out to be one of the busiest."	Opinion	This statement shows that the author believes Paul Revere was busy all his life. She seems to be very impressed by him.
264		Opinion	
266		Fact	
269		Fact	
275		Opinion and Fact	

Name _____

When Did It Happen, Paul Revere?

**The timeline below lists some important dates in Paul Revere's life.
Answer the questions next to each date to help complete the
timeline.**

1735 — What is Boston like when Paul Revere is born?

_____

_____

1756 — How does Revere respond when French soldiers and Indians attack the
colonies?

_____

1773 — On the night of December 16, Revere and the other Sons of Liberty are
very busy in Boston Harbor. What are they doing?

_____

_____

1776 — On the night of April 18, Revere is sent to Lexington and Concord.
What happens on his Big Ride?

_____

_____

_____

1783 — By the end of the war, Revere is 48 years old. What does he do?

_____

_____

1810 — What is Boston like now that Revere is 75 years old?

_____

_____

Name _____

Viewing the Author

Read the passage. Then answer the questions on page 199.

Traitor or Hero?

How should Benedict Arnold be remembered: as a traitor, or as a hero of the American Revolution? I'm not sure this question has a simple answer.

Arnold joined the Patriot militia in 1774. After the Revolutionary War began in 1775, he helped lead the capture of Fort Ticonderoga from the British. Later that year, he led over a thousand soldiers into Canada, was wounded in battle, and earned a promotion for bravery. In October of 1777, he was again seriously wounded as he led his soldiers against the forces of the British general Burgoyne. Arnold's courageous leadership helped the Americans win one of their most important victories in the war.

But in 1780, Arnold worked out a plan with the British to surrender an important American military base in exchange for money. After his plan was discovered, he escaped and joined the British army. Why did he do this? Many historians believe that Arnold felt his country had treated him unfairly. He was disappointed when he was passed over for a promotion. He was also accused of being too easy on Americans who were loyal to the British. This may have angered him.

The British never paid Arnold all the money he asked for. The land they gave him in Canada was not useful to him. When Arnold died in 1801, he had become poor, discouraged, and lonely, for he was a man few people trusted. Arnold was a traitor, it is true. But we should not forget that he performed several heroic acts that helped our nation win its independence.

Name _____

Viewing the Author continued

1. What is the viewpoint of the author of this passage?

   _____

   _____

2. Which sentences reveal the author's viewpoint?

   _____

   _____

3. What do you think the author's purpose is for writing this passage?

   _____

   _____

4. Write a sentence from the passage that shows the author's opinion.

   _____

   _____

5. Write a fact from the passage that helps to support the author's viewpoint.

   _____

   _____

6. Write a fact from the passage that might support a different viewpoint about the subject.

   _____

   _____

   _____

   _____

   _____

Name _____

No Apostrophes!

Your school is putting on a play of *And Then What Happened, Paul Revere?* You're sending an e-mail to the script writer, but the apostrophe (') on the computer doesn't work! Change each contraction or possessive to its longer form. Write P for possessive or C for contraction in each box.

1. Paul makes a squirrel's silver collar.
   _____ ☐

2. The writing's sloppy in the letters Paul writes.
   _____ ☐

3. Paul rings the church bells at a moment's notice.
   _____ ☐

4. The English are taxing tea, glass, and printers' inks.
   _____ ☐

5. Paul doesn't miss a chance to help the Sons of Liberty.
   _____ ☐

6. A messenger's job is to travel from place to place on horseback.
   _____ ☐

7. Cloth to cover the oars isn't all Paul leaves behind.
   _____ ☐

8. He goes back to rescue the Patriots' papers.
   _____ ☐

Name _____

Final /ər/

The **schwa sound** is a weak vowel sound that is often found in an unstressed syllable. It is shown as /ə/. When you hear the final /ər/ sound in words of more than one syllable, think of the patterns *er*, *or*, and *ar*.

/ər/ ang**er**, act**or**, pill**ar**

Write each Spelling Word under the pattern that spells its final /ər/ sound.

1. theater
2. actor
3. mirror
4. powder
5. humor
6. anger
7. banner
8. pillar
9. major
10. thunder
11. flavor
12. finger
13. mayor
14. polar
15. clover
16. burglar
17. tractor
18. matter
19. lunar
20. quarter

er

_____
_____
_____
_____
_____
_____
_____
_____

or

_____
_____
_____
_____
_____
_____

ar

_____
_____
_____

Name _____

Spelling Spree

Find a Rhyme For each sentence write a Spelling Word
that rhymes with the underlined word and makes sense.

1. Do me a <u>favor</u> and pick a different _____ of ice cream.
2. I <u>wonder</u> if we'll hear _____ during the rainstorm.
3. The town paved <u>over</u> a field of _____.
4. The butler hung a colorful _____ outside the <u>manor</u>.
5. Put the _____ in the coin <u>sorter</u>.
6. They hope to run the _____ station on <u>solar</u> power.
7. The _____ was a <u>factor</u> in the movie's success.

1. _____   5. _____
2. _____   6. _____
3. _____   7. _____
4. _____

Puzzle Play Write the Spelling Word that fits each clue. Then
write the circled letters in order below.

8. a farm machine

9. a pointer or a pinky

10. fury

11. a column

12. a thief

13. a surface that reflects

14. place for movies

15. person in charge of a city

Mystery Words: a

Spelling Words

1. theater
2. actor
3. mirror
4. powder
5. humor
6. anger
7. banner
8. pillar
9. major
10. thunder
11. flavor
12. finger
13. mayor
14. polar
15. clover
16. burglar
17. tractor
18. matter
19. lunar
20. quarter

Name _____

Proofreading and Writing

Proofreading Circle the five misspelled Spelling Words in this
notice to British troops. Then write each word correctly.

April 16, 1775

From Boston Headquarters:

*We are planning a majer march into the
countryside on the evening of the 18th. The
current lunor phase will give us a full moon, so
there will be plenty of light. If all goes well, we
will surprise the rebels and take their supplies of
guns and powdur. This mater should be kept
secret, of course. Stay calm, and react to any
unpleasant situations with humer rather than
anger. More details will follow.*

1. theater
2. actor
3. mirror
4. powder
5. humor
6. anger
7. banner
8. pillar
9. major
10. thunder
11. flavor
12. finger
13. mayor
14. polar
15. clover
16. burglar
17. tractor
18. matter
19. lunar
20. quarter

1. _____   4. _____

2. _____   5. _____

3. _____

✏️➤ **Write Interview Questions** If you could interview Paul Revere,
what questions would you ask him? Would you like to know more
about his work as a silversmith or details of his famous ride?

**On a separate piece of paper, write some questions that you would
like to ask this famous patriot about his life and the historical events
in which he took part. Use Spelling Words from the list.**

Name _____

Synonym Switch

Find a synonym in the box for each underlined word.
Rewrite the sentences using the synonyms.

1. In Boston Harbor, ships constantly <u>came</u> and <u>left</u>.

   _____

   _____

2. Paul <u>found</u> that money could be <u>made</u> in many ways.

   _____

   _____

3. The men <u>hauled</u> the chests to the deck and <u>tossed</u> the tea overboard.

   _____

   _____

4. Paul <u>slipped</u> past the sentries and <u>dashed</u> through the snow.

   _____

   _____

5. Paul <u>beat</u> on doors in Lexington and <u>aroused</u> the citizens.

   _____

   _____

Vocabulary

arrived

departed

discovered

dragged

earned

hurried

pounded

sneaked

threw

woke

Name _____

Where's Your House, Paul Revere?

Subject-Verb Agreement A verb must agree in number with its subject. In the present tense, add *-s* or *-es* to the verb if the subject is singular. Do not add *-s* or *-es* if the subject is plural or if the subject is *I* or *you*. If you are using *be* or *have* as helping verbs, use the form that agrees with the subject in number.

Complete each sentence with the present-tense form of the verb in parentheses that agrees with the subject in number.

1. We _____ visiting Paul Revere's house in Boston. (be)

2. My cousin _____ the silver teapot on display. (like)

3. I _____ tankards Paul Revere made. (see)

4. A 900-pound bell _____ in the courtyard of the Revere house. (stand)

5. The silver cup and tray _____ brightly. (shine)

6. You _____ to the Old North Church. (walk)

7. She _____ gazing at the church steeple where the lanterns hung. (be)

8. I _____ Revere's midnight ride to Lexington. (imagine)

9. Tourists _____ the Freedom Trail in Boston. (walk)

10. I _____ learned about American patriots. (have)

Name _____

What Was Your Ride Like, Paul Revere?

Regular and Irregular Verbs To form the past tense of regular verbs, add -*ed* to the verb. Irregular verbs have special forms for the past tense. Do not add -*ed* to irregular verbs.

Tracy and Kim have written an interview to perform in history class. To enjoy the interview, fill in the correct past-tense forms of the verbs in parentheses. You may have to check irregular verbs in your dictionary.

Reporter: We are on the scene with the famous Patriot Paul Revere. Mr. Revere, you have returned from an important mission. What was it like on that ride, sir?

Paul Revere: My midnight ride _____ (be) exciting. I _____ (ride) as fast as I _____ (can)! I don't think I have ever _____ (ride) so fast before!

Reporter: We have heard that you _____ (forget) your spurs. Is that true?

Paul Revere: Yes, I _____ (do), but my faithful dog _____ (bring) them to me.

Reporter: You also _____ (row) across the river, right?

Paul Revere: I _____ (run) as fast as I could, too, and I _____ (warn) the people about the British.

Reporter: Paul Revere, American Patriot, your country is grateful.

Name _____

What Did You See, Shirley Jensen?

Choosing the Correct Verb Form It is important for a writer to choose the correct form of a verb. For irregular verbs, you may have to check your dictionary.

Shirley keeps a journal on her computer. She recently took a trip to Boston and wants to write an essay about her experience. To get started, she has printed out her journal entries. Proofread the journal entry below and circle the incorrect verb forms. Then write the correct form above the error.

July 15

We arrived at Logan Airport this morning. We taked a subway to Grandma's apartment in Boston. I had took a subway train before in New York City. I wish we haved a subway in Allentown!

Grandma fixes us lunch, but I wasn't hungry because I had ate too many peanuts on the plane. I thinked we might go to the beach in the afternoon, but we goed downtown instead. Grandma shown us the State House with the golden dome. It was beautiful! Then we visit Paul Revere's house. We seen some of the beautiful things he made.

Name _____

Writing a Character Sketch

And Then What Happened, Paul Revere? gives many details about Paul Revere, a hero of the American Revolution. These details help you understand what he did and what kind of person he was. Using vivid details in your writing can help bring a real person like Paul Revere or a story character to life.

A **character sketch** is a written profile that describes how a real person or a story character looks, acts, thinks, and feels.

Choose a real person or a story character from another selection you have read whom you think would make a good subject for a character sketch. Then use the web to brainstorm details about the character's physical appearance and personality traits.

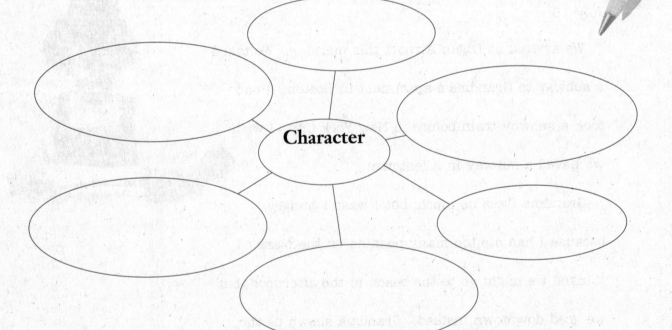

On a separate sheet of paper, write your character sketch. Begin with a quote or an anecdote about the character. Then write a sentence that summarizes his or her most significant character traits. Next, give two or three details from the web that support your summary. Finally, conclude by restating the character's most significant traits.

Name _____

Using Exact Nouns and Verbs

Which noun, *lights* or *chandeliers*, is more exact? Which verb, *galloped* or *rode*, is more exact? A good writer avoids using vague nouns and verbs. Exact nouns and verbs like *chandeliers* and *galloped* can make your writing clearer and help readers create a more vivid mental picture of the people, places, and events that you describe.

One fifth-grader drafted these sentences for a character sketch about Paul Revere. Can you help her make her writing clearer and more vivid? Rewrite each sentence on the lines, replacing the underlined vague nouns and verbs with more exact ones from the list below.

More Exact Nouns and Verbs

crafted	careers
hardware store	colonists
opened	warned
tea	silver
pursued	dumped

1. Throughout his life, Paul Revere <u>did</u> many different <u>things</u>.

_____

_____

2. He <u>made</u> pitchers, candlesticks, and buckles from <u>metal</u>.

_____

_____

3. With other patriots, he disguised himself as an Indian, boarded a British ship, and <u>put</u> <u>stuff</u> into Boston Harbor.

_____

_____

4. He became a hero when he <u>told</u> <u>people</u> that British troops were coming.

_____

_____

Name _____

Revising Your Story

Reread your story. Put a checkmark in the box for each sentence that describes your paper. Use this page to help you revise.

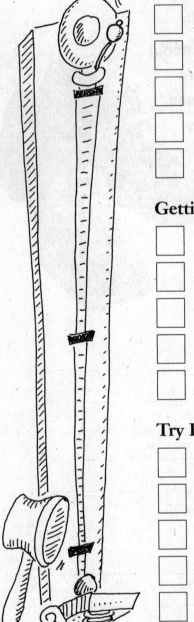

Rings the Bell

☐ My setting, characters, and plot are well developed.

☐ The beginning, middle, and end are clear. Events are in order.

☐ My writing creates a particular mood for my story.

☐ Details, exact words, and dialogue bring my story to life.

☐ Sentences flow smoothly. There are very few mistakes.

Getting Stronger

☐ The setting, characters, and plot could be more interesting.

☐ Parts of the story are missing. Some events are out of order.

☐ My story does not sound the way I want it to.

☐ More details, exact words, and dialogue are needed.

☐ Sentences flow smoothly. There are a few mistakes.

Try Harder

☐ There is no setting or plot. My characters are flat.

☐ There is no beginning or ending. The order is confusing.

☐ You can't hear my voice. My story has no particular mood.

☐ There are no details or exact words. I didn't use dialogue.

☐ Sentences are short or unclear, with many mistakes.

Name _____

Using Exact Verbs

Replace each underlined verb. Circle the letter of the verb that best completes each sentence.

1. Nina <u>rearranged</u> the cards in the deck.

   a. moved   b. mixed   c. shuffled   d. wrinkled

2. "<u>Have</u> one card," she said to Ted. "Then put it back into the deck."

   a. Replace   b. Remove   c. Repair   d. Deliver

3. "Is this your card?" she asked, <u>showing</u> the Queen of Hearts.

   a. flashing   b. flushing   c. hiding   d. presenting

4. Ted <u>moved</u> his head sadly. "No, it's not my card," he said.

   a. rotated   b. turned   c. stiffened   d. shook

5. "Oh goodness," Nina said. "I've <u>done it</u> again."

   a. smiled   b. misjudged   c. blundered   d. coughed

6. Then Nina's hand <u>went</u> behind her ear and pulled out a card.

   a. fell   b. darted   c. skipped   d. grasped

7. "That's my card," Ted <u>said</u>. "The deuce of clubs!"

   a. mentioned   b. noted   c. exclaimed   d. whispered

8. "Thank you very much," Nina said. She bowed to her audience and <u>ran</u> off the stage.

   a. scampered   b. slinked   c. wriggled   d. skipped

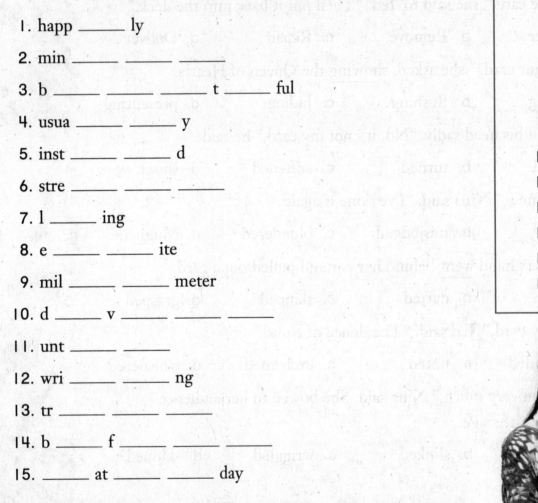

Name _____

Spelling Words

Words Often Misspelled Look for familiar spelling patterns to help you remember how to spell the Spelling Words on this page. Think carefully about the parts that you find hard to spell in each word.

Write the missing letters in the Spelling Words below.

1. happ _____ ly

2. min _____ _____ _____

3. b _____ _____ _____ t _____ ful

4. usua _____ _____ y

5. inst _____ _____ d

6. stre _____ _____ _____

7. l _____ ing

8. e _____ _____ ite

9. mil _____ _____ meter

10. d _____ v _____ _____ _____

11. unt _____ _____

12. wri _____ _____ ng

13. tr _____ _____ _____

14. b _____ f _____ _____ _____

15. _____ at _____ _____ day

Spelling Words

1. happily
2. minute
3. beautiful
4. usually
5. instead
6. stretch
7. lying
8. excite
9. millimeter
10. divide
11. until
12. writing
13. tried
14. before
15. Saturday

Study List **On a separate piece of paper, write each Spelling Word. Check your spelling against the words on the list.**

Spelling Spree

Phrase Fillers Write the Spelling Word that best completes
each phrase.

1. a _____ and true method

2. to yawn and _____

3. wait a _____

4. _____ down for a nap

5. to _____ into two pieces

6. dinner comes _____ dessert

7. _____ a letter

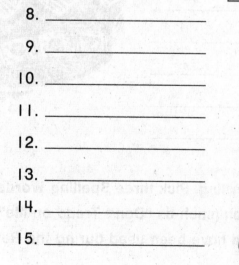

Spelling Words

1. happily
2. minute
3. beautiful
4. usually
5. instead
6. stretch
7. lying
8. excite
9. millimeter
10. divide
11. until
12. writing
13. tried
14. before
15. Saturday

1. _____

2. _____

3. _____

4. _____

5. _____

6. _____

7. _____

Syllable Scramble Rearrange the syllables to write a
Spelling Word. One syllable in each item is extra.

8. til un till

9. ur date day Sat

10. cite ite ex

11. ly u al fer su

12. pi hap an ly

13. in ted stead

14. ti ness ful beau

15. mil time ter li me

8. _____

9. _____

10. _____

11. _____

12. _____

13. _____

14. _____

15. _____

Proofreading and Writing

Proofreading Circle the five misspelled Spelling Words in this open letter. Then write each word correctly.

Fellow Countrymen:

I am riting these words to urge you all to action. This land cannot spend another minut under the tyrannical rule of the British King! We have tride to plead and reason with him, but he will not listen. Now, insted of talking, we must fight! If we do, it will not be long before we are living hapilly in our own nation. Join the struggle for liberty now!

Spelling Words

1. happily
2. minute
3. beautiful
4. usually
5. instead
6. stretch
7. lying
8. excite
9. millimeter
10. divide
11. until
12. writing
13. tried
14. before
15. Saturday

1. _____
2. _____
3. _____
4. _____
5. _____

Slogan Writing Pick three Spelling Words. Then, with each one, write a slogan (such as "Don't Tread on Me" or "Liberty or Death") that could have been used during the Revolutionary War.

Name _____

Some Talk of Revolution

Answer each of the following questions by writing a vocabulary word.

Vocabulary

arming

skittish

just

fierce

skirmish

peered

rebels

kin

drilling

1. Which word means "right" or "fair"?

   _____

2. Which word names individuals fighting against their

   government? _____

3. Which word means "giving weapons to"?

   _____

4. Which word means "practicing for battle"?

   _____

5. Which word is a synonym for *nervous*?

   _____

6. Which word means "looked"?

   _____

7. Which word is an antonym for *meek*?

   _____

8. Which word means "a brief battle"?

   _____

9. Which word is a synonym for *relatives*?

   _____

Write a different question using one of the vocabulary words.

_____

_____

Name _____

Why Did It Happen?

Fill in the columns where indicated with the cause or the effect of the events included in the chart.

Causes	Effects
_____ _____ _____	The uneasiness and fighting make Katie's family feel skittish, nervous, and worried.
_____ _____ _____	The family has lost friends and neighbors.
Armed rebels come to Katie's home.	_____ _____
Katie feels that it is not just for their neighbors to break into their house and ruin their things.	_____ _____
_____ _____ _____	Katie hides inside her mother's wedding trunk.
When John Warren searches the trunk and discovers Katie, he calls the rebels away and leaves the lid open so she can breathe.	_____ _____ _____

216   Theme 3: **Voices of the Revolution**

Name _____

In the Characters' Words

Read the characters' words in the left column. In the right column, write why each character said what he or she did.

What the Character Said	Why the Character Said It
Mama: "It makes me as skittish as a newborn calf."	_____ _____ _____
Papa: "Get your mother! Hide in the woods."	_____ _____ _____
Katie: "It was not right. It was not just. It was not fair."	_____ _____ _____
The rebels: "This'll be fine pickings!"	_____ _____ _____
John Warren: "Out! The Tories are coming. Back to the road! Hurry!"	_____ _____ _____
Katie: "He'd left one seam of goodness there, and we were all tied to it."	_____ _____ _____

Name _____

Making Connections

Read the story. Then complete the activity on page 219.

A Dangerous Day

My name is Margaret Tompkins. I work as a nurse in a field hospital here in Virginia. When my brother enlisted as a soldier in the Continental army, I, too, wanted to join and help the cause. I decided to become a nurse. I came to this area three months ago when my brother's company was sent here.

For the past few hours, our soldiers have been involved in a fierce battle. After almost ten hours of fighting, they are exhausted and very hungry. Some of the wounded have been brought to the hospital, where the other nurses and I have been treating them. It is hard, heartbreaking work.

It is now just past three in the afternoon. Over the noise, I suddenly hear my brother's voice calling "Margaret!" I grab a medical bag and run out onto the field. When I reach James, he is sitting next to a cannon, holding his left shoulder.

"What has happened?" I ask him.

"The cannon recoiled and twisted my shoulder out of its socket," he tells me. I tell James I will lead him to the hospital so he can be treated. He shakes his head. "I can't leave here," he says. "Someone has to fire the cannon."

I look around and realize that, for the moment, no one else is nearby. Finally I say, "James, you cannot fire a cannon with a dislocated shoulder. You go. I have watched cannons being fired. I'll take a turn here." He goes.

I feel afraid. But I prepare the cannon. Here is a chance to do more to win the war than just unroll bandages.

Making Connections continued

Complete the cause-effect chain to show what caused the events described on page 218, and what happened as a result.

Causes	Effects
Margaret wants to help the Patriot effect.	_____ _____ _____
_____ _____	Margaret travels to Virginia to work in a field hospital and be near him.
_____ _____	James's shoulder is dislocated.
James refuses to get his shoulder treated because he is the only soldier at the post.	_____ _____ _____
_____ _____ _____	Margaret prepares the cannon even though she feels afraid.

Name _____

Signalling Syllables

Rewrite each underlined word, adding slashes between its syllables.
Then write a definition of the word.

1. The family usually sat and talked with visitors in the <u>parlor</u>.

   _____

2. Katie's mother is <u>skittish</u> because of the fighting in the area.

   _____

3. <u>Dragonflies</u> would land briefly on the rocks before flying away again.

   _____

4. As she hid in the trunk, Katie heard <u>faraway</u> voices and footsteps.

   _____

5. The incident was just a <u>skirmish</u>, not a major battle.

   _____

6. A large horse went <u>thudding</u> by on the road.

   _____

Name _____

VCCV and VCV Patterns

A **syllable** is a word part with one vowel sound. To spell a two-syllable word, divide the word into syllables. Divide a VCCV word between the consonants. Divide a VCV word before or after the consonant. Look for spelling patterns you have learned, and spell the word by syllables.

VC | CV	VC | CV
ar | rive	**par | lor**
VC | V	V | CV
val | ue	**a | ware**
clos | et	**be | have**

Write each Spelling Word under the heading that tells how it is divided.

Spelling Words

1. equal
2. parlor
3. collect
4. closet
5. perhaps
6. wedding
7. rapid
8. value
9. arrive
10. behave
11. shoulder
12. novel
13. tulip
14. sorrow
15. vanish
16. essay
17. publish
18. aware
19. subject
20. prefer

VC | CV

_____

_____

_____

_____

_____

_____

_____

VC | V

_____

_____

_____

V | CV

_____

_____

_____

_____

_____

Spelling Spree

Syllable Match Match each of the following syllables with one
of the numbered syllables to create Spelling Words. Then
write the words on the blanks provided.

ar	qual	have	par	a
et	wed	pre	lish	el

1. **nov** _____

2. **lor** _____

3. **fer** _____

4. **clos** _____

5. **e** _____

6. **ding** _____

7. **be** _____

8. **ware** _____

9. **rive** _____

10. **pub** _____

The Third Word Write the Spelling Word that
belongs with each group.

11. sadness, grief, _____

12. possibly, maybe, _____

13. worth, price, _____

14. gather, accumulate, _____

15. fast, speedy, _____

16. rose, daffodil, _____

17. topic, field, _____

18. paper, report, _____

19. wrist, elbow, _____

20. fade, disappear, _____

Name _____

Proofreading and Writing

Proofreading Circle the five misspelled Spelling Words in this speech. Then write each word correctly.

Fellow Townspeople!

Recent events have made it clear. The flag of England will soon vannish from our land. We are aware, however, that certain people prefur to remain loyal to King George. This has made some of us angry. Indeed, some people behav as if they don't know their own neighbors. The rappid changes of the past months have stirred up strong feelings, but everyone must remain calm! If you vallue the freedoms of our new land, you will respect your neighbors' homes and property whether or not you share their beliefs.

Spelling Words

1. equal
2. parlor
3. collect
4. closet
5. perhaps
6. wedding
7. rapid
8. value
9. arrive
10. behave
11. shoulder
12. novel
13. tulip
14. sorrow
15. vanish
16. essay
17. publish
18. aware
19. subject
20. prefer

1. _____   4. _____

2. _____   5. _____

3. _____

✎➤ **Write a Bulletin-Board Notice** You want your classmates to join you in some activity, perhaps organizing a pep rally or raising money for disaster relief or some other worthy cause. How will you get their attention?

On a separate piece of paper, write a notice to tack up on a school bulletin board giving reasons why students should join you in the activity.

Name _____

Turning the Key

Use the spelling table/pronunciation key to figure out how to
pronounce the underlined words. Then find a word in the
box with the same vowel sound as the underlined word, and
write it after the sentence.

Vocabulary

> meant
> steer
> blood
> took
> town
> flour

Sounds	Spellings	Sample Words
/ĕ/	e, ea	shed, breath
/î/	ea, ee, ie, e	dear, deer, pier, mere
/ŭ/	o, u, ou, oo	cut, rough, flood
/o͝o/	u, oo, o	full, book, wolf
/ou/	ou, ow	about, crown

1. <u>Crouched</u> in the underbrush, I felt like an animal in a trap.

_____

2. In a <u>fierce</u> whisper, Mama was trying to call me back.

_____

3. The men ripped the knocker off the <u>wood</u>.

_____

4. The rustle of the clothing in the trunk <u>drowned</u> their words.

_____

5. I could hear the <u>drums</u> of the rebels who were marching in

town.

_____

6. A sudden <u>thread</u> of a song ran through my head.

_____

Name _____

Katie's Adventure

Verb Phrases with *have* Many verb phrases begin with a form of *have*, *has*, or *had*. Use *has* with singular subjects. Use *have* with plural subjects or with *I* or *you*. Use *had* with either singular subjects or plural subjects.

Underline the verb phrase in the following sentences.

1. Katie and her family had been friends with their neighbors before the revolution.

2. Political differences now have come between them.

3. It has been difficult for everyone.

4. The rebels have entered the house.

5. Katie has hidden in a trunk.

Fill in the correct form of the verbs in parentheses to complete the following sentences.

6. They have _____ (break) a precious teapot.

7. It has _____ (be) a trying time for the family.

8. I have _____ (enjoy) reading the story about British loyalists.

9. You have _____ (make) me think.

10. Mr. Roby had _____ (hope) the class would like the story.

Name _____

Let Us Learn About Lexington

teach, learn; let, leave; sit, set; can, may Some pairs of verbs can be confusing. The meanings of these verbs are related but different. Study the definitions carefully.

teach—to instruct

learn—to be instructed

sit—to rest or stay in one place

set—to put

let—to allow

leave—to go away

can—to have the ability to

may—to have permission

Choose between the two verbs in parentheses to correctly complete each sentence.

1. We will _____ (teach, learn) about the American Revolution.

2. Ms. Amata will _____ (teach, learn) us about the Tories.

3. In Lexington, our class _____ (can, may) see a statue of a Minuteman.

4. You _____ (can, may) take my picture beside the statue.

5. In Boston, we _____ (can, may) see the harbor where the rebels dumped the tea.

6. We will _____ (sit, set) on a bench at the harbor.

7. I'll _____ (sit, set) my camera on the bench.

8. _____ (Can, May) I borrow your history book?

9. My teacher _____ (lets, leaves) me ask many questions.

10. They will _____ (let, leave) before lunch.

Name _____

Uncle Warren's Trunk

Choosing the Correct Verb Michael is writing a letter to his cousin, but he is uncertain about the correct verb to use. Choose the correct verbs from the list to fill in the blanks.

teach
learn
let
leave
sit
set
can
may

Dear Kenya,

　　I read a story about a girl who had to hide in a trunk. It reminded me of the trunk we saw in Uncle Warren's attic. Do you remember? I talked to Uncle Warren on Sunday, and he said that we _____ open it next time we visit. I hope we find a Revolutionary War sword inside! If we do, we _____ try to find out who owned it. We would _____ a lot about history that way. Uncle Warren doesn't think we will find anything that old, but he said he will _____ us about the history of our family.

　　_____ you come next Saturday? If not, will your parents _____ you come the following Saturday? If you _____ your house before noon, we _____ have lunch. I will _____ on the porch and wait for you. I better _____ down my pen now and turn out the light.

　　　　　　Your cousin,
　　　　　　Michael

Name _____

Writing a Friendly Letter

Katie Gray in *Katie's Trunk* lived in the 1700s during the Revolutionary War — long before the invention of either the telephone or the computer. If she wanted to share her experience of hiding in the trunk, Katie could not have called a friend or sent an e-mail message. However, she might have written a friendly letter.

A **friendly letter** is a letter that you write to a friend to share news about your life.

Use this page to help you plan and organize a friendly letter. Either write to a friend of yours, or write a letter that Katie might have written to a friend. Use a separate sheet of paper, and follow these steps:

1. Write a **heading** (your address and the date) in the upper right corner.

2. Write a **greeting** (*Dear* and the person's name followed by a comma) at the left margin.

3. Write the **body** of your letter below the greeting. Begin by writing something that demonstrates you care about your friend. Include your personal thoughts, feelings, or news. Make sure to use a friendly tone and informal language. At the end of the letter, ask your friend to write back soon.

4. Write an informal **closing** such as *Love* or *Your friend* followed by a comma in the lower right corner.

5. Sign your name under the closing.

When your friendly letter is finished, address an envelope and mail it or share it with a classmate.

Name _____

Voice

Every writer has a **voice,** or a unique way of expressing himself or herself. A writer's voice helps reveal what he or she is like as a person. You can sometimes also "hear" a narrator's or a character's voice when you read a work of literature. For example, listen for Mama's voice as you read this sentence from *Katie's Trunk:* "Tea! In the harbor! Wasting God's good food."

You can strengthen your own writing voice when you write by showing more of what you think and feel, and by including expressions you commonly use when speaking, such as *No way!* or *I'm psyched* or *You've got to be kidding.*

On the lines below, write ten expressions that you commonly use when speaking.

My Common Expressions

_____
(expression of fear)

_____
(expression of disgust)

_____
(expression of surprise)

_____
(expression of embarrassment)

_____
(expression of encouragement)

_____
(expression of affection)

_____
(expression of confusion)

_____
(expression of pleasure)

_____
(expression of doubt)

_____
(expression of concern)

When you revise your friendly letter, use these expressions to strengthen your writing voice. By adding a few of these expressions, you can make your writing sound more natural — as if you are talking directly to your friend.

Name _____

Drama on the High Seas

Complete each sentence below by writing a vocabulary word from the box.

1. Those opposing slavery were called _____.

2. A group whose views are respected by leaders is considered
   to be _____.

3. If you have helped a person, you have
   _____ him or her.

4. An argument is one type of _____.

5. Changing direction while sailing is _____.

6. If you have told a group that their plan seems solid, you have
   _____ them to carry it out.

7. Another word for *prisoners* is _____.

8. If you feel strong fear, you feel _____.

9. _____ is preventing people from living
   in freedom.

10. A _____ was a private ship given papers
    by a government allowing it to attack ships of another country.

11. A person learning a trade is an _____.

Choose one of the vocabulary words and write a sentence.

_____

_____

Name _____

James Forten and the Revolutionary War

Complete the chart as you read the selection.

What I Know	What I Want to Know	What I Learned
_____	_____	_____
_____	_____	_____
_____	_____	_____
_____	_____	_____
_____	_____	_____
_____	_____	_____
_____	_____	_____
_____	_____	_____
_____	_____	_____
_____	_____	_____
_____	_____	_____
_____	_____	_____
_____	_____	_____
_____	_____	_____
_____	_____	_____
_____	_____	_____
_____	_____	_____

Name _____

Did It Really Happen?

The sentences below tell about James Forten. Write T if the sentence is true, or F if the sentence is false. If a sentence is false, correct it to make it true.

1. _____ New York, where James Forten was born, was home to many significant abolitionists.

   _____

   _____

2. _____ James became a foot soldier when he was 14 years old.

   _____

   _____

3. _____ On his second voyage, James Forten and the crew of the *Royal Louis* were captured and held captive on board the British prison ship *Jersey*.

   _____

   _____

4. _____ James feared he would be killed by the British.

   _____

   _____

5. _____ It was probably George Washington's victory over the British that saved Forten.

   _____

   _____

6. _____ After the war, James Forten became a wealthy politician and an influential abolitionist.

   _____

   _____

Name _____

Step by Step

Read the directions. Then answer the questions on page 234.

"Wild Snake" Marble Game

This marble game provides good marble-shooting practice.

Players: Two or more

Materials: One marble per player; a stick or a piece of chalk

Object: The winner is the last player left in the game.

How to Play:

1. If the game is played on sand, scratch seven circles to form a course. If it is played on cement, draw seven circles with chalk. The course may go in any direction.

2. Make a starting line and place all players' marbles behind it.

3. Taking turns, players try to land their marble in the first circle by flicking it with their thumb or finger.

4. A player who lands a marble in the first circle proceeds to the second one, and so on.

5. A player who gets to the seventh circle must complete the course in reverse.

6. Players who complete the course forward and backward are "wild snakes." This means that they may shoot at the other players' marbles.

7. If a player's marble is hit by the marble of a wild snake, that player is out of the game (even if that player is also a wild snake).

8. If a wild snake's marble lands in a circle while trying to shoot another player's marble, the wild snake is out of the game.

Name _____

Step by Step continued

Answer these questions about the directions on page 233.

1. What do the directions teach readers?

_____

_____

2. In order to follow these directions, what should you do first?

_____

_____

3. What does each player need before play can begin?

_____

_____

4. Why do you need chalk if you are playing the game on cement?

_____

_____

5. How does a player become a "wild snake"?

_____

_____

6. What can cause a wild snake to be out of the game?

_____

_____

7. What would happen if you did step number two before doing step
number one?

_____

_____

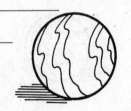

Name _____

Prefix Plus

**Use the charts to figure out the meaning of each underlined word.
Then rewrite the word in the blank space, using the clues. The first
one has been done for you.**

Prefix	Meaning
sub-	under, below
sur-	over, above

Word Root	Meaning
mit	to cause to go
ject	to throw
vey	to look
merge	to plunge

Base Words
mount (climb)
standard (usual quality)
face (part)
pass

1. The rebels would not <u>submit</u> to unfair British laws.

   The rebels would not _____go under_____ unfair British laws.

2. The naval officer <u>surveyed</u> the harbor.

   The naval officer _____ the harbor.

3. A harbor seal <u>submerged</u> near the ship.

   A harbor seal _____ near the ship.

4. Soon, the seal came to the <u>surface</u> of the ocean.

   Soon, the seal came to the _____ of the ocean.

5. The prisoners were <u>subjected</u> to punishment.

   The prisoners were _____ punishment.

6. James thought the tattered sailcloth was <u>substandard</u>.

   James thought the tattered sailcloth was _____.

7. With his positive attitude, James could <u>surmount</u> any problem.

   James could _____ any problem.

8. James's sails <u>surpassed</u> any others.

   James's sails _____ any others.

Name _____

Final /l/ or /əl/

The final /l/ or /əl/ sounds are usually spelled with two letters. When you hear these sounds, think of the patterns *le*, *el*, and *al*.

/l/ or /əl/   spark**le**, jew**el**, leg**al**

► The spellings of *fossil* and *devil* differ from the usual spelling patterns. The /əl/ sounds in these words are spelled *il*.

Write each Spelling Word under its spelling of the final /l/ or /əl/ sound.

le

_____

_____

_____

_____

_____

_____

al

_____

_____

Another Spelling

_____

_____

el

_____

_____

_____

_____

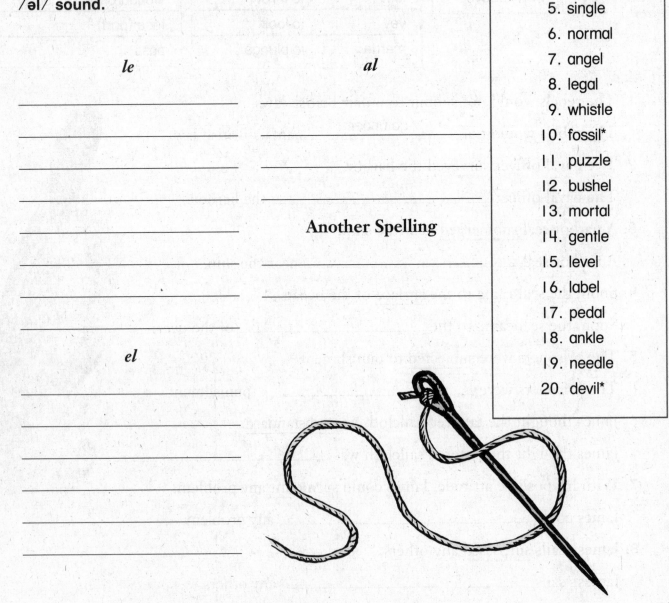

Name _____

Spelling Spree

Ending Match For each beginning syllable, choose the correct spelling of the /l/ or /əl/ sound to form a Spelling Word. Then write each word correctly.

1. spar-   -kel   -kle   -kal   1. _____

2. gen-   -tle   -tal   -til   2. _____

3. fos-   -sle   -sal   -sil   3. _____

4. puz-   -zel   -zle   -el   4. _____

5. la-   -bel   -bal   -ble   5. _____

6. whis-   -tel   -tle   -tal   6. _____

7. mor-   -tle   -tel   -tal   7. _____

Crack the Code Some Spelling Words have been written in the following code. Use the code to figure out each word. Then write each word correctly.

CODE:	R	E	N	O	T	V	A	G	B	F	Y	M
LETTER:	A	D	E	G	I	J	K	L	N	P	V	W

8. RBAGN   _____

9. GNYNG   _____

10. RBONG   _____

11. BNNEGN   _____

12. RBOGN   _____

13. VNMNG   _____

14. ENYTG   _____

15. FNERG   _____

Spelling Words

1. jewel
2. sparkle
3. angle
4. shovel
5. single
6. normal
7. angel
8. legal
9. whistle
10. fossil*
11. puzzle
12. bushel
13. mortal
14. gentle
15. level
16. label
17. pedal
18. ankle
19. needle
20. devil*

Theme 3: **Voices of the Revolution**   237

Name _____

Proofreading and Writing

Proofreading Circle the five misspelled Spelling Words in the following Help Wanted advertisement. Then write each word correctly.

> **Are you tired** of doing dirty work with a shovle? Maybe you're sick of hauling bushal baskets of vegetables to market. We're looking for a hard-working, singel young man or woman to be an apprentice in the sailmaking business. You must be of legil working age, and you should be willing to work with a large needle.
>
> **Please apply in person during normel business hours at the office of James Forten, Sailmaker.**

1. _____   4. _____

2. _____   5. _____

3. _____

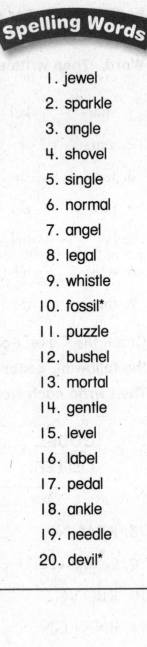

✎ **Write a Character Sketch** James Forten had an unusual life. At various times he was a sailor in the Revolutionary War, a sailmaker, a successful businessman, and an abolitionist. Is there anything about his personality that you think would have helped him in the different parts of his life?

On a separate sheet of paper, write a brief character sketch of James Forten. Use Spelling Words from the list.

Name _____

Journal of Opposites

Read the journal. In each blank, write an antonym of the clue word.

December 31, 1781

This summer I set sail aboard the *Royal Louis*. We were ready to

fight the _____ British navy. Soon we were caught up
(powerless)

in battle with the _____ armed ship *Active*. I carried
(lightly)

gunpowder from _____ the decks to the guns. In time,
(above)

the *Active* surrendered by _____ its flag. I'll never
(raising)

forget the crowd's excited _____ as we took the ship
(booing)

back to Philadelphia. But our next trip out was _____.
(lucky)

Our ship surrendered to three British ships, and we crew members were

_____ as prisoners. At least the boys were
(set free)

_____ to play marbles. The captain's son joined us,
(forbidden)

and we became _____. I wonder if this friendship
(enemies)

saved me from being _____ into slavery.
(bought)

Name _____

What Kind? How Many? Which One?

Adjectives A word that describes a noun or a pronoun is called an **adjective**. It tells what kind or how many. *A*, *an*, and *the* are special adjectives called **articles**. *A* and *an* refer to any item. *The* refers to a particular item. *This*, *that*, *these*, and *those* are **demonstrative adjectives**. They tell which one. *This* and *these* refer to nearby items; *that* and *those* refer to farther away items.

Circle all of the adjectives in the following sentences, including articles and demonstrative adjectives.

1. James sewed straight seams on large, square sails.

2. Those ships needed many sails.

3. Six sailors are pulling on the thick ropes.

4. This huge vessel is impressive.

5. Tired merchants closed the shops.

6. Grateful citizens will raise a cheer for these sailors.

7. An anchor is thrown overboard.

8. A white seagull dives for the slippery fish.

9. That shop sells sails and other equipment for ships.

10. Philadelphia has a proud heritage.

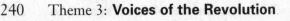

Name _____

Who Settled Where?

Proper Adjectives A **proper adjective** is formed from a proper noun and always begins with a capital letter.

Fill in the blank with the proper adjective formed from the proper noun in parentheses. Check a dictionary if you need to. (Number four is tricky!)

1. The state of Louisiana was once a _____ colony. (France)

2. The _____ Revolution was a fight for independence from England. (America)

3. King George III sat on the _____ throne. (England)

4. There were _____ settlers in New York. (Holland)

5. _____ explorers settled parts of Florida. (Spain)

6. Margaret's _____ ancestors settled in Pennsylvania. (Germany)

7. Many _____ immigrants came to America in the nineteenth century. (Ireland)

8. James Forten's ancestors were _____. (Africa)

9. Alaska was once a _____ territory. (Russia)

10. General Washington fought _____ soldiers. (Britain)

Name _____

Marvelous Marbles

Expanding Sentences with Adjectives Good writers add interest to their writing by adding adjectives that help readers visualize a scene.

Add adjectives to the following sentences to make them more lively and interesting. Use your imagination!

1. These _____ children are playing with marbles.

2. That _____ bag holds _____ marbles.

3. Alfred sits on the _____ ground to play.

4. Carla shows Tony a _____ marble.

5. The players enjoy the _____ sunshine.

6. Kinley doesn't play marbles, but he collects _____ cards.

7. That _____ girl usually wins.

8. The _____ boy in the _____ jacket won today!

Name _____

Writing a Biography

In *James Forten*, you read about an African American sailor who served during the Revolutionary War. A **biography** is a written account of important events and significant experiences in a person's life. Before you write a biography of your own, follow these steps:

► Choose a real person whom you admire or a person who lived during the American Revolution.

► Research important facts, dates, places, events, and accomplishments in this person's life. Use the Internet, reference books, or history books in your library to gather information.

Record and organize important dates, locations, and events in this person's life on the timeline below.

The Life of _____

DATE	EVENT
_____	
_____	
_____	
_____	

Now write your biography on a separate sheet of paper. Start with an anecdote or a famous quotation from this person's life. Then work from your timeline. Write about important events and experiences, using chronological order, time-order words, and key dates. Highlight the events that you think best reveal this person's character or major accomplishments. Finally, conclude by summarizing why this person is remembered.

Name _____

Capitalizing Names of People and Places

Good biographers proofread their writing to check for correct capitalization of proper names. Imagine you have written a biography of James Forten. The book jacket will include information to interest readers in the book.

Proofread the following book-jacket sentences. Underline the names of people and places that should be capitalized and write them correctly on the lines.

African American sailor james forten was born in philadelphia in 1766.

_____

Living on the shores of the atlantic ocean, he dreamed of glory on the high seas.

_____

When he was only fourteen years old, he joined the crew of a vessel that was commanded by captain stephen decatur.

_____

The *royal louis* was a privateer, or a privately owned ship that the united states used in the war against england.

_____

After the British captured his ship in 1781, the teenaged sailor was imprisoned in the filthy hold of a prison ship, the *jersey*, which was anchored off new york.

_____

This young patriot feared little — except the bitter chance that he would be sent to the west indies and enslaved.

_____

Name _____

Code Words

Use the words in the box to complete the sentences below.

Vocabulary

retreats   intend   courier   timid   suspect

Write the words next to their definitions. Unscramble the circled letters to answer the question that follows.

1. to mistrust ☐☐☐☐◯☐☐

2. to plan to do something ☐☐☐☐☐◯ to do

3. person who delivers messages ◯☐◯☐☐☐☐

4. shy or frightened ☐☐☐☐◯

5. times when an army runs away from an attack
☐☐☐☐☐◯☐☐☐

What do you do to a secret message to read it?

☐☐☐☐☐☐

Name _____

Effective Spies

After reading each selection, complete the chart below to show what you learned.

Toliver's Secret	
Cause	**Effect**
Ellen's grandfather has hurt his ankle.	
	Ellen looks like a boy.

Mary Redmond, John Darragh, and Dicey Langston: Spies	
Cause	**Effect**
Mary Redmond sees two British soldiers eyeing her partner.	
	The British soldiers at the checkpoint do not find the messages John Darragh is carrying.

Mood Chart

Use the chart below to compare and contrast the moods in *Toliver's Secret* and *And Then What Happened, Paul Revere?*

Toliver's Secret

Page 334B: *And then the British army came to New York and there had been three months of defeat. "If you understand how important it is to take the message, Ellen, I'll tell you how it can be done. And then you are to decide." Ellen listened and didn't say a word.*	Mood Created: _____ Key Words and Phrases: _____ _____ _____ _____
Page 334F: *She ran into the shop to show her grandfather how she looked. For the first time since he fell on the ice, Grandfather laughed. "You look like a ragged little urchin all right," he said, "with those holes in your elbows. But all the better. No one will even notice you."*	Mood Created: _____ Key Words and Phrases: _____ _____ _____ _____

And Then What Happened, Paul Revere?

Page 269: *From Boston to Cambridge to Watertown to Worcester to Hartford (Watch out, dogs on the road! Watch out, chickens!) to New York to Philadelphia he went. And back. 63 miles a day. (This was not swatting flies!)*	Mood Created: _____ Key Words and Phrases: _____ _____ _____ _____
Page 273: *And then suddenly from out of the shadows appeared six English officers. They rode up with their pistols in their hands and ordered Paul to stop. But Paul didn't stop immediately. "Stop!" one of the officers shouted. "If you go an inch farther, you are a dead man."*	Mood Created: _____ Key Words and Phrases: _____ _____ _____ _____

Name _____

Vocabulary Match

For each item, circle the letter of the answer that best fits the underlined vocabulary word.

1. The spy searched the market and tried to spot his <u>contacts</u>.
   A. friends   C. students
   B. connections   D. soldiers

2. The woman tried to look <u>casual</u> as she handed off the secret message.
   A. happy   C. sad
   B. not concerned   D. dangerous

3. The message was <u>encoded</u> so that the British would not be able to read it.
   A. unclear   C. written with secret symbols
   B. listened to   D. read aloud

4. The spy secretly stuffed the message in his shoe, knowing he would be in great <u>peril</u> if anyone saw him.
   A. water   C. danger
   B. safety   D. confusion

5. Now he had to cross a river full of British boats, and he <u>steeled</u> himself for this terrifying trip.
   A. doubted   C. strengthened
   B. talked to   D. weakened

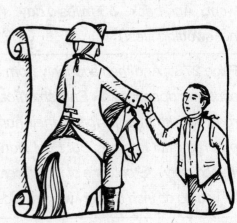

Name _____

Test Practice

Use the three steps you've learned to write a personal response to these questions about *Mary Redmond, John Darragh, and Dicey Langston: Spies.* **Make a chart on a separate paper. Then write your response on the lines below.**

1. Would you have done what Mary, John, or Dicey did? Explain why you would or would not risk your life as they did.

_____

_____

_____

_____

_____

_____

_____

_____

_____

_____

_____

_____

_____

Personal Response Checklist

✔ Did I restate the question at the beginning?

✔ Can I add more details from what I read to support my answer?

✔ Can I add more of my thoughts or experiences to support my answer?

✔ Do I need to delete any details that do not help answer the question?

✔ Where can I add more exact words?

✔ Did I use clear handwriting? Did I make any mistakes?

Continue on page 250.

Test Practice continued

2. **Connecting/Comparing** Both Dicey Langston and James Forten show courage. Besides courage, what qualities do you most admire in both Dicey and James? Why do you admire these qualities?

_____

_____

_____

_____

_____

_____

_____

_____

_____

_____

_____

_____

Personal Response Checklist

✔ Did I restate the question at the beginning?

✔ Can I add more details from what I read to support my answer?

✔ Can I add more of my thoughts or experiences to support my answer?

✔ Do I need to delete any details that do not help answer the question?

✔ Where can I add more exact words?

✔ Did I use clear handwriting? Did I make any mistakes?

Read your answers to Questions 1 and 2 aloud to a partner. Then discuss the questions on the checklist. Make any changes that will improve your answers.

Name _____

Author's Viewpoint

Read the paragraph below. Then answer the questions.

George Washington was a most remarkable man. He is truly worthy of the title "Father of the Country." First, Washington led the army that defeated the British during the Revolutionary War. He then served as a leader of the effort to write the United States Constitution. As if that weren't enough, he went on to serve as the new country's first President.

1. What is the author's viewpoint of George Washington?

   _____

2. What words reveal the author's opinions about Washington?

   _____

3. What facts does the author include in support of his or her viewpoint?

   _____

   _____

   _____

Name _____

Follow the Steps

Read the directions. Then answer the questions below.

How to Carry a Secret Message

What You'll Need: pen or pencil, sheet of paper, large loaf of unsliced bread, bread knife, handkerchief

Steps:

1. Write your secret message on the paper.
2. Fold the paper into a small square or rectangle. It should be half the width of the loaf of bread.
3. Carefully cut a rectangle in the bottom of the loaf of bread. Make sure the slice you cut doesn't break.
4. Place the message inside the space in the loaf.
5. Put the slice back into the space.
6. Wrap the loaf in a handkerchief so that the message is on the bottom.

Now you are ready to deliver your message.

1. What do the directions show how to do?

_____

2. To follow these directions correctly, what is the first thing you should do?

_____

3. What materials do you need to gather before you begin?

_____

4. Why do you have to make sure that the slice of bread you cut doesn't break?

_____

5. What would happen if you did Step 5 before Step 4?

_____

Name _____

Match Words and Meanings

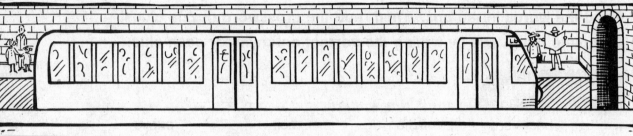

Read the sentences. Then read the definitions. Draw a line from each sentence to the definition that goes with the underlined word.

1. Will the climbers <u>surmount</u> the peak before nightfall?

2. The <u>submarine</u> dove deep beneath the surface.

3. We should explore the tide pools only after the big waves <u>subside</u>.

4. They hope to <u>surpass</u> the current record very soon.

5. Riding the <u>subway</u> is the fastest way to get downtown.

6. Any <u>surplus</u> canned food can be donated to the shelter.

7. The <u>surcharge</u> on each ticket is $1.75.

8. They plan to <u>subdivide</u> the land into four smaller plots.

a. "sink down to a lower level"

b. "amount beyond what is needed"

c. "added amount that must be paid"

d. "a ship that goes underwater"

e. "make into smaller pieces"

f. "a train that travels underground"

g. "go to the top of"

h. "go beyond"

Name _____

Antonym Crossword

Read the words in the box. Then read the crossword puzzle clues.
Complete the puzzle by writing the correct antonym for each clue.

Word Bank

backward	fiction	melt	public
deep	forget	plain	start
difficult	laugh	problem	wild

Across

1. easy
4. cry
6. fancy
7. tame
9. solution
11. finish

Down

1. shallow
2. fact
3. private
5. forward
8. remember
10. freeze

Name _____

Spelling Review

**Write Spelling Words from the list on this page to answer the
questions.**

1–12. Which twelve words have the final /ər/ sounds?

1. _____   7. _____

2. _____   8. _____

3. _____   9. _____

4. _____   10. _____

5. _____   11. _____

6. _____   12. _____

13–23. Which eleven words have the final /l/ or /əl/ sounds?

13. _____   19. _____

14. _____   20. _____

15. _____   21. _____

16. _____   22. _____

17. _____   23. _____

18. _____

24–30. What syllable is missing from each word? Write
each word.

24. sor— _____   28. —ware _____

25. —have _____   29. —ue _____

26. wed— _____   30. pub— _____

27. rap— _____

Spelling Words

1. jewel
2. polar
3. needle
4. humor
5. legal
6. mayor
7. gentle
8. lunar
9. sorrow
10. tractor
11. quarter
12. behave
13. parlor
14. wedding
15. powder
16. actor
17. rapid
18. equal
19. mortal
20. aware
21. matter
22. sparkle
23. shoulder
24. bushel
25. value
26. publish
27. single
28. whistle
29. burglar
30. pedal

Name _____

Spelling Spree

Syllable Rhymes Write the Spelling Word that has a first syllable that rhymes with each word below.

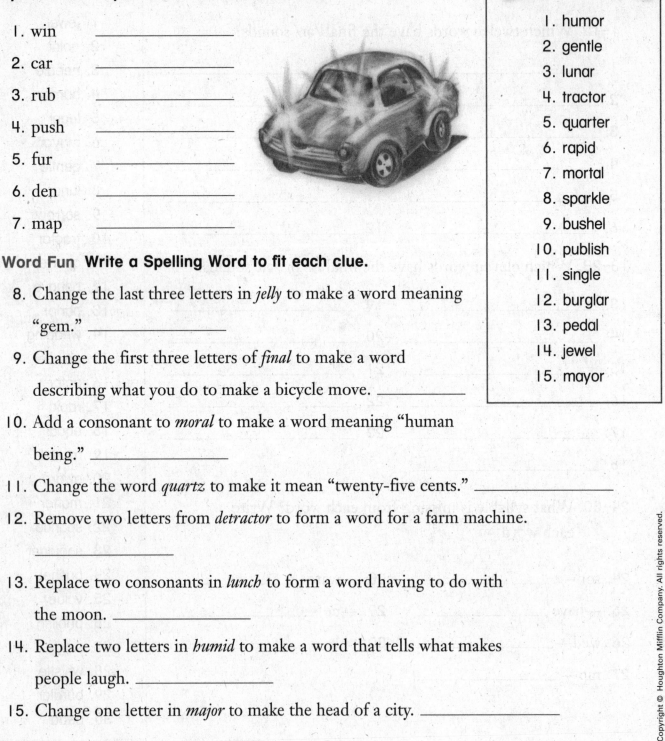

1. win   _____

2. car   _____

3. rub   _____

4. push   _____

5. fur   _____

6. den   _____

7. map   _____

Spelling Words

1. humor
2. gentle
3. lunar
4. tractor
5. quarter
6. rapid
7. mortal
8. sparkle
9. bushel
10. publish
11. single
12. burglar
13. pedal
14. jewel
15. mayor

Word Fun Write a Spelling Word to fit each clue.

8. Change the last three letters in *jelly* to make a word meaning "gem." _____

9. Change the first three letters of *final* to make a word describing what you do to make a bicycle move. _____

10. Add a consonant to *moral* to make a word meaning "human being." _____

11. Change the word *quartz* to make it mean "twenty-five cents." _____

12. Remove two letters from *detractor* to form a word for a farm machine.

    _____

13. Replace two consonants in *lunch* to form a word having to do with the moon. _____

14. Replace two letters in *humid* to make a word that tells what makes people laugh. _____

15. Change one letter in *major* to make the head of a city. _____

Name _____

Proofreading and Writing

Proofreading **Circle the five misspelled Spelling Words in this report. Then write each word correctly.**

Betsy Ross sat in her parler with a few scraps of cloth, a needel, and some thread. She usually made jackets, weding dresses, and lacy shirts. That day, she made a flag with great valyew for the new nation. It made the colonial army equel to the British.

1. _____   4. _____

2. _____   5. _____

3. _____

Title Trouble **Correct the following book titles. Replace each underlined word with a rhyming Spelling Word.**

6. *Soldiers, Keep Your <u>Chowder</u> Close By* _____

7. *Just <u>Thistle</u>, I'll Come Running!* _____

8. *The <u>Factor</u> Who Makes History Come Alive* _____

9. *One Soldier's <u>Borrow</u>; Another's Joy* _____

10. *Be <u>Compare</u> of Danger Signs* _____

11. *Manners: How a Soldier Should <u>Shave</u>* _____

12. *Valley Forge—Cold as <u>Solar</u> Ice* _____

13. *He Carried His Musket on His <u>Boulder</u>* _____

14. *The New Flag Really Does <u>Flatter</u>!* _____

15. *The <u>Regal</u> Papers* _____

✏ **Write a Diary Entry** **On a separate sheet of paper, write a diary entry telling about a colonial American's day. Use the Spelling Review Words.**

Spelling Words

1. powder
2. polar
3. matter
4. parlor
5. equal
6. aware
7. behave
8. sorrow
9. shoulder
10. value
11. whistle
12. needle
13. legal
14. actor
15. wedding

Theme 3: **Voices of the Revolution**   257

Name _____

Making Verbs Agree with Subjects

Complete each sentence with a present tense form of the verb in parentheses. Be sure it agrees with the subject in number.

1. The girl _____ a short haircut. (have)

2. Her cap _____ red with white stripes. (be)

3. Mittens _____ her hands warm. (keep)

4. Warm corncakes _____ delicious. (smell)

5. Her grandfather _____ given her a hidden message. (have)

6. A messenger _____ severe punishment. (risk)

7. The local boatmen _____ kindly. (be)

8. Friends _____ the girl at a tavern. (await)

9. Coins _____ in the girl's pocket. (jingle)

10. The girl _____ a deep breath. (take)

Writing Past Tense Verbs

Complete each sentence. Use the past tense form of the verb in parentheses. You may need to check irregular verbs in your dictionary.

1. A farmer _____ his boat across the water. (row)

2. He _____ a rope from the boat to the dock. (tie)

3. He _____ a Patriot near the marketplace. (meet)

4. The Patriot _____ the farmer a packet. (give)

5. The farmer _____ the packet in the lining of his coat. (hide)

6. The farmer _____ the Patriot's hand. (squeeze)

7. He _____ a basket of vegetables to the marketplace. (bring)

8. The farmer _____ the vegetables to a friend. (sell)

9. They _____ about the progress of the Revolution. (talk)

10. Then he _____ to his boat with the hidden message. (return)

Student Handbook

Contents

How to Study a Word

1. LOOK at the word.
➤ What does the word mean?
➤ What letters are in the word?
➤ Name and touch each letter.

2. SAY the word.
➤ Listen for the consonant sounds.
➤ Listen for the vowel sounds.

3. THINK about the word.
➤ How is each sound spelled?
➤ Close your eyes and picture the word.
➤ What familiar spelling patterns do you see?
➤ Did you see any prefixes, suffixes, or other word parts?

4. WRITE the word.
➤ Think about the sounds and the letters.
➤ Form the letters correctly.

5. CHECK the spelling.
➤ Did you spell the word the same way it is spelled in your word list?
➤ If you did not spell the word correctly, write the word again.

accept	buy	friend		
ache	by	goes		
again	calendar	going	ninth	tried
all right	cannot	grammar	often	tries
almost	can't	guard	once	truly
already	careful	guess	other	two
although	catch	guide	people	unknown
always	caught	half	principal	until
angel	chief	haven't	quiet	unusual
angle	children	hear	quit	wasn't
answer	choose	heard	quite	wear
argue	chose	heavy	really	weather
asked	color	height	receive	Wednesday
aunt	cough	here	rhythm	weird
author	cousin	hers	right	we'll
awful	decide	hole	Saturday	we're
babies	divide	hoping	stretch	weren't
been	does	hour	surely	we've
believe	don't	its	their	where
bother	early	it's	theirs	which
bought	enough	January	there	whole
break	every	let's	they're	witch
breakfast	exact	listen	they've	won't
breathe	except	loose	those	wouldn't
broken	excite	lose	though	write
brother	expect	minute	thought	writing
brought	February	muscle	through	written
bruise	finally	neighbor	tied	you're
build	forty	nickel	tired	yours
business	fourth	ninety	to	
busy	Friday	ninety-nine	too	

Eye of the Storm

The /ā/, /ē/, and /ī/ Sounds
/ā/ → m**a**le, cl**ai**m, str**ay**
/ē/ → l**ea**f, fl**ee**t
/ī/ → str**ike**, th**igh**, s**ign**

Spelling Words

1. speech
2. claim
3. strike
4. stray
5. fade
6. sign
7. leaf
8. thigh
9. thief
10. height
11. mild
12. waist
13. sway
14. beast
15. stain
16. fleet
17. stride
18. praise
19. slight
20. niece

Challenge Words

1. campaign
2. describe
3. cease
4. sacrifice
5. plight

My Study List
Add your own
spelling words
on the back. ➡

Nature's Fury
Reading-Writing
Workshop

Look for familiar spelling patterns in these words to help you remember their spellings.

Spelling Words

1. enough
2. caught
3. brought
4. thought
5. every
6. ninety
7. their
8. they're
9. there
10. there's
11. know
12. knew
13. o'clock
14. we're
15. people

Challenge Words

1. decent
2. stationery
3. stationary
4. correspond
5. reversible

My Study List
Add your own
spelling words
on the back. ➡

Earthquake Terror

Short Vowels
/ă/ → st**a**ff
/ĕ/ → sl**e**pt
/ĭ/ → m**i**st
/ŏ/ → d**o**ck
/ŭ/ → b**u**nk

Spelling Words

1. bunk
2. staff
3. dock
4. slept
5. mist
6. bunch
7. swift
8. stuck
9. breath
10. tough
11. fond
12. crush
13. grasp
14. dwell
15. fund
16. ditch
17. split
18. swept
19. deaf
20. rough

Challenge Words

1. trek
2. frantic
3. summit
4. rustic
5. mascot

My Study List
Add your own
spelling words
on the back. ➡

Take-Home Word List

Name _____

My Study List

1. _____
2. _____
3. _____
4. _____
5. _____
6. _____
7. _____
8. _____
9. _____
10. _____

Review Words

1. trunk
2. skill
3. track
4. fresh
5. odd

How to Study a Word

Look at the word.
Say the word.
Think about the word.
Write the word.
Check the spelling.

266

Take-Home Word List

Name _____

My Study List

1. _____
2. _____
3. _____
4. _____
5. _____
6. _____
7. _____
8. _____
9. _____
10. _____

How to Study a Word

Look at the word.
Say the word.
Think about the word.
Write the word.
Check the spelling.

266

Take-Home Word List

Name _____

My Study List

1. _____
2. _____
3. _____
4. _____
5. _____
6. _____
7. _____
8. _____
9. _____
10. _____

Review Words

1. free
2. twice
3. gray
4. least
5. safe

How to Study a Word

Look at the word.
Say the word.
Think about the word.
Write the word.
Check the spelling.

266

Michelle Kwan: Heart of a Champion

Compound Words
wheel + chair =
  wheelchair
up + to + date =
  up-to-date
first + aid = first aid

Spelling Words

1. basketball
2. wheelchair
3. cheerleader
4. newscast
5. weekend
6. everybody
7. up-to-date
8. grandparent
9. first aid
10. wildlife
11. highway
12. daytime
13. whoever
14. test tube
15. turnpike
16. shipyard
17. homemade
18. household
19. salesperson
20. brother-in-law

Challenge Words

1. extraordinary
2. self-assured
3. quick-witted
4. limelight
5. junior high school

My Study List
Add your own
spelling words
on the back. ➡

Nature's Fury Spelling Review

Spelling Words

1. slept
2. split
3. staff
4. fade
5. praise
6. slope
7. claim
8. stroll
9. mood
10. beast
11. crush
12. fond
13. dwell
14. strike
15. clue
16. boast
17. flute
18. sway
19. cruise
20. mild
21. grasp
22. swift
23. bunk
24. slight
25. thrown
26. stole
27. fleet
28. dew
29. youth
30. thigh

See the back for Challenge Words.

My Study List
Add your own
spelling words
on the back. ➡

Volcanoes

The /ō/, /o͞o/, and /yo͞o/ Sounds
/ō/ ➡ st**o**le, b**oa**st, thr**ow**n, str**o**ll
/o͞o/ or ➡ r**u**le, cl**u**e,
/yo͞o/ d**ew**, m**oo**d, cr**u**ise, r**ou**te

Spelling Words

1. thrown
2. stole
3. clue
4. dew
5. choose
6. rule
7. boast
8. cruise
9. stroll
10. route
11. mood
12. loaf
13. growth
14. youth
15. slope
16. bruise
17. loose
18. rude
19. flow
20. flute

Challenge Words

1. subdue
2. pursuit
3. molten
4. reproach
5. presume

My Study List
Add your own
spelling words
on the back. ➡

Take-Home Word List

Take-Home Word List

Take-Home Word List

Name _____

Name _____

Name _____

My Study List

1. _____
2. _____
3. _____
4. _____
5. _____
6. _____
7. _____
8. _____
9. _____
10. _____

My Study List

1. _____
2. _____
3. _____
4. _____
5. _____
6. _____
7. _____
8. _____
9. _____
10. _____

My Study List

1. _____
2. _____
3. _____
4. _____
5. _____
6. _____
7. _____
8. _____
9. _____
10. _____

Review Words

1. group
2. goal
3. fruit
4. blew
5. broke

Challenge Words

1. frantic
2. trek
3. cease
4. molten
5. pursuit
6. rustic
7. describe
8. campaign
9. subdue
10. reproach

Review Words

1. afternoon
2. ninety-nine
3. everywhere
4. all right
5. breakfast

How to Study a Word

Look at the word.
Say the word.
Think about the word.
Write the word.
Check the spelling.

How to Study a Word

Look at the word.
Say the word.
Think about the word.
Write the word.
Check the spelling.

How to Study a Word

Look at the word.
Say the word.
Think about the word.
Write the word.
Check the spelling.

The Fear Place

The /ôr/, /âr/, and /är/ Sounds

/ôr/ → torch, soar, sore
/âr/ → hare, flair
/är/ → scar

Spelling Words

1. hare
2. scar
3. torch
4. soar
5. harsh
6. sore
7. lord
8. flair
9. warn
10. floor
11. tore
12. lair
13. snare
14. carve
15. bore
16. fare
17. gorge
18. barge
19. flare
20. rare

Challenge Words

1. folklore
2. unicorn
3. ordinary
4. marvelous
5. hoard

My Study List
Add your own spelling words on the back. ➡

La Bamba

The /ou/, /ô/, and /oi/ Sounds

/ou/ → ounce, tower
/ô/ → claw, pause, bald
/oi/ → moist, loyal

Spelling Words

1. hawk
2. claw
3. bald
4. tower
5. halt
6. prowl
7. loyal
8. pause
9. moist
10. ounce
11. launch
12. royal
13. scowl
14. haunt
15. noisy
16. coward
17. fawn
18. thousand
19. drown
20. fault

Challenge Words

1. announce
2. poise
3. loiter
4. somersault
5. awkward

My Study List
Add your own spelling words on the back. ➡

Give It All You've Got!
Reading-Writing Workshop

Look for familiar spelling patterns in these words to help you remember their spellings.

Spelling Words

1. would
2. wouldn't
3. clothes
4. happened
5. someone
6. sometimes
7. different
8. another
9. weird
10. eighth
11. coming
12. getting
13. going
14. stopped
15. here

Challenge Words

1. irresponsible
2. affectionate
3. brilliance
4. audible
5. menace

My Study List
Add your own spelling words on the back. ➡

Take-Home Word List

Name _____

My Study List

1. _____
2. _____
3. _____
4. _____
5. _____
6. _____
7. _____
8. _____
9. _____
10. _____

How to Study a Word

Look at the word.
Say the word.
Think about the word.
Write the word.
Check the spelling.

Take-Home Word List

Name _____

My Study List

1. _____
2. _____
3. _____
4. _____
5. _____
6. _____
7. _____
8. _____
9. _____
10. _____

Review Words

1. proud
2. dawn
3. false
4. cause
5. howl

How to Study a Word

Look at the word.
Say the word.
Think about the word.
Write the word.
Check the spelling.

Take-Home Word List

Name _____

My Study List

1. _____
2. _____
3. _____
4. _____
5. _____
6. _____
7. _____
8. _____
9. _____
10. _____

Review Words

1. horse
2. sharp
3. square
4. stairs
5. board

How to Study a Word

Look at the word.
Say the word.
Think about the word.
Write the word.
Check the spelling.

And Then What Happened, Paul Revere?

Final /ər/

/ər/ → ang**er**, act**or**
pill**ar**

Spelling Words

1. theater
2. actor
3. mirror
4. powder
5. humor
6. anger
7. banner
8. pillar
9. major
10. thunder
11. flavor
12. finger
13. mayor
14. polar
15. clover
16. burglar
17. tractor
18. matter
19. lunar
20. quarter

Challenge Words

1. oyster
2. clamor
3. tremor
4. scholar
5. chamber

My Study List
Add your own spelling words on the back. →

Give It All You've Got!
Spelling Review

Spelling Words

1. weekend
2. hawk
3. flair
4. stir
5. first aid
6. halt
7. royal
8. carve
9. worth
10. hurl
11. up-to-date
12. noisy
13. soar
14. barge
15. steer
16. wildlife
17. coward
18. gorge
19. return
20. smear
21. brother-in-law
22. thousand
23. tore
24. early
25. pearl
26. test tube
27. launch
28. snare
29. perch
30. wheelchair

See the back for Challenge Words.

My Study List
Add your own spelling words on the back. →

Mae Jemison

The /ûr/ and /îr/ Sounds

/ûr/ → g**er**m, st**ir**, ret**ur**n, **ear**ly, w**or**th

/îr/ → p**eer**, sm**ear**

Spelling Words

1. smear
2. germ
3. return
4. peer
5. stir
6. squirm
7. nerve
8. early
9. worth
10. pier
11. thirst
12. burnt
13. rear
14. term
15. steer
16. pearl
17. squirt
18. perch
19. hurl
20. worse

Challenge Words

1. interpret
2. yearn
3. emergency
4. dreary
5. career

My Study List
Add your own spelling words on the back. →

Take-Home Word List

Name _____

My Study List

1. _____
2. _____
3. _____
4. _____
5. _____
6. _____
7. _____
8. _____
9. _____
10. _____

Review Words

1. learn
2. curve
3. world
4. firm
5. year

How to Study a Word

Look at the word.
Say the word.
Think about the word.
Write the word.
Check the spelling.

Take-Home Word List

Name _____

My Study List

1. _____
2. _____
3. _____
4. _____
5. _____
6. _____
7. _____
8. _____
9. _____
10. _____

Challenge Words

1. extra-ordinary
2. announce
3. loiter
4. marvelous
5. yearn
6. self-assured
7. somersault
8. ordinary
9. emergency
10. dreary

How to Study a Word

Look at the word.
Say the word.
Think about the word.
Write the word.
Check the spelling.

Take-Home Word List

Name _____

My Study List

1. _____
2. _____
3. _____
4. _____
5. _____
6. _____
7. _____
8. _____
9. _____
10. _____

Review Words

1. enter
2. honor
3. answer
4. collar
5. doctor

How to Study a Word

Look at the word.
Say the word.
Think about the word.
Write the word.
Check the spelling.

James Forten

Final /l/ or /əl/

| /l/ or | sparkle, |
| /əl/ → | jewel, legal |

Spelling Words

1. jewel
2. sparkle
3. angle
4. shovel
5. single
6. normal
7. angel
8. legal
9. whistle
10. fossil
11. puzzle
12. bushel
13. mortal
14. gentle
15. level
16. label
17. pedal
18. ankle
19. needle
20. devil

Challenge Words

1. mineral
2. influential
3. vital
4. neutral
5. kernel

My Study List
Add your own spelling words on the back. ➡

273

Katie's Trunk

VCCV and VCV Patterns

VC|CV	VC|V	V|CV
ar|rive	val|ue	tu|lip
par|lor	clos|et	a|ware
		be|have

Spelling Words

1. equal
2. parlor
3. collect
4. closet
5. perhaps
6. wedding
7. rapid
8. value
9. arrive
10. behave
11. shoulder
12. novel
13. tulip
14. sorrow
15. vanish
16. essay
17. publish
18. aware
19. subject
20. prefer

Challenge Words

1. device
2. skittish
3. logic
4. sincere
5. nuisance

My Study List
Add your own spelling words on the back. ➡

273

Voices of the Revolution
Reading-Writing Workshop

Look for familiar spelling patterns in these words to help you remember their spellings.

Spelling Words

1. happily
2. minute
3. beautiful
4. usually
5. instead
6. stretch
7. lying
8. excite
9. millimeter
10. divide
11. until
12. writing
13. tried
14. before
15. Saturday

Challenge Words

1. fatigue
2. antique
3. accumulate
4. camouflage
5. tongue

My Study List
Add your own spelling words on the back. ➡

273

Take-Home Word List

Name _____

My Study List

1. _____
2. _____
3. _____
4. _____
5. _____
6. _____
7. _____
8. _____
9. _____
10. _____

How to Study a Word

Look at the word.
Say the word.
Think about the word.
Write the word.
Check the spelling.

Take-Home Word List

Name _____

My Study List

1. _____
2. _____
3. _____
4. _____
5. _____
6. _____
7. _____
8. _____
9. _____
10. _____

Review Words

1. person
2. mistake
3. human
4. bottom
5. stomach

How to Study a Word

Look at the word.
Say the word.
Think about the word.
Write the word.
Check the spelling.

Take-Home Word List

Name _____

My Study List

1. _____
2. _____
3. _____
4. _____
5. _____
6. _____
7. _____
8. _____
9. _____
10. _____

Review Words

1. simple
2. special
3. metal
4. nickel
5. double

How to Study a Word

Look at the word.
Say the word.
Think about the word.
Write the word.
Check the spelling.

Voices of the Revolution
Spelling Review

Spelling Words

1. powder	16. humor
2. burglar	17. behave
3. rapid	18. quarter
4. value	19. whistle
5. bushel	20. needle
6. actor	21. mayor
7. equal	22. sorrow
8. publish	23. parlor
9. tractor	24. mortal
10. pedal	25. gentle
11. polar	26. lunar
12. aware	27. shoulder
13. matter	28. jewel
14. single	29. legal
15. sparkle	30. wedding

**See the back for
Challenge Words.**

My Study List
Add your own
spelling words
on the back. ➡

Name _____

My Study List

1. _____
2. _____
3. _____
4. _____
5. _____
6. _____
7. _____
8. _____
9. _____
10. _____

Challenge Words

1. oyster
2. skittish
3. influential
4. kernel
5. clamor
6. device
7. mineral
8. vital
9. sincere
10. scholar

How to Study a Word

Look at the word.
Say the word.
Think about the word.
Write the word.
Check the spelling.

276

Focus on Tall Tales

**Vowel Changes:
Long to Short**
A long vowel sound may be
spelled the same as a short
vowel sound in words that
are related in meaning.

Spelling Words

1. steal	11. crime
2. stealth	12. criminal
3. cave	13. breathe
4. cavity	14. breath
5. wise	15. wild
6. wisdom	16. wilderness
7. deal	17. shade
8. dealt	18. shadow
9. athlete	19. revise
10. athletic	20. revision

Challenge Words

1. volcano
2. volcanic
3. cycle
4. bicycle

My Study List
Add your own
spelling words
on the back. ➡

Focus on Poetry

Homophones
Homophones are words
that sound the same but
have different spellings and
meanings.

Spelling Words

1. cord	11. role
2. chord	12. roll
3. pray	13. peel
4. prey	14. peal
5. seam	15. shone
6. seem	16. shown
7. sole	17. pain
8. soul	18. pane
9. piece	19. pole
10. peace	20. poll

Challenge Words

1. aisle
2. isle
3. rein
4. reign

My Study List
Add your own
spelling words
on the back. ➡

Name _____

My Study List

1. _____
2. _____
3. _____
4. _____
5. _____
6. _____
7. _____
8. _____
9. _____
10. _____

Review Words

1. final
2. finish
3. heal
4. health

How to Study a Word

Look at the word.
Say the word.
Think about the word.
Write the word.
Check the spelling.

Name _____

My Study List

1. _____
2. _____
3. _____
4. _____
5. _____
6. _____
7. _____
8. _____
9. _____
10. _____

Review Words

1. hall
2. haul
3. dear
4. deer

How to Study a Word

Look at the word.
Say the word.
Think about the word.
Write the word.
Check the spelling.

Problem Words

Words	Rules	Examples
bad badly	*Bad* is an adjective. It can be used after linking verbs like *look* and *feel*. *Badly* is an adverb.	This was a <u>bad</u> day. I feel <u>bad</u>. I play <u>badly</u>.
borrow lend	*Borrow* means "to take." *Lend* means "to give."	You may <u>borrow</u> my pen. I will <u>lend</u> it to you for the day.
can may	*Can* means "to be able to do something." *May* means "to be allowed or permitted."	Nellie <u>can</u> read quickly. May I borrow your book?
good well	*Good* is an adjective. *Well* is usually an adverb. It is an adjective only when it refers to health.	The weather looks <u>good</u>. She sings <u>well</u>. Do you feel <u>well</u>?
in into	*In* means "located within." *Into* means "movement from the outside to the inside."	Your lunch is <u>in</u> that bag. He jumped <u>into</u> the pool.
its it's	*Its* is a possessive pronoun. *It's* is a contraction of *it is*.	The dog wagged <u>its</u> tail. <u>It's</u> cold today.
let leave	*Let* means "to permit or allow." *Leave* means "to go away from" or "to let remain in place."	Please <u>let</u> me go swimming. I will <u>leave</u> soon. <u>Leave</u> it on my desk.
lie lay	*Lie* means "to rest or recline." *Lay* means "to put or place something."	The dog <u>lies</u> in its bed. Please <u>lay</u> the books there.

Problem Words continued

Words	Rules	Examples
sit set	*Sit* means "to rest in one place." *Set* means "to place or put."	Please <u>sit</u> in this chair. <u>Set</u> the vase on the table.
teach learn	*Teach* means "to give instruction." *Learn* means "to receive instruction."	He <u>teaches</u> us how to dance. I <u>learned</u> about history.
their there they're	*Their* is a possessive pronoun. *There* is an adverb. It may also begin a sentence. *They're* is a contraction of *they are*.	<u>Their</u> coats are on the bed. Is Carlos <u>there</u>? <u>There</u> is my book. <u>They're</u> going to the store.
two to too	*Two* is a number. *To* means "in the direction of." *Too* means "more than enough" and "also."	I bought <u>two</u> shirts. A squirrel ran <u>to</u> the tree. May we go <u>too</u>?
whose who's	*Whose* is a possessive pronoun. *Who's* is a contraction for *who is*.	<u>Whose</u> tickets are these? <u>Who's</u> that woman?
your you're	*Your* is a possessive pronoun. *You're* is a contraction for *you are*.	Are these <u>your</u> glasses? <u>You're</u> late again!

Read each question below. Then check your paper. Correct any mistakes you find. After you have corrected them, put a check mark in the box next to the question.

☐   1. Did I spell all the words correctly?

☐   2. Did I indent each paragraph?

☐   3. Does each sentence state a complete thought?

☐   4. Are there any run-on sentences or fragments?

☐   5. Did I begin each sentence with a capital letter?

☐   6. Did I capitalize all proper nouns?

☐   7. Did I end each sentence with the correct end mark?

☐   8. Did I use commas, apostrophes, and quotation marks correctly?

Are there other problem areas you should watch for? Make your own proofreading checklist.

☐ _____

☐ _____

☐ _____

☐ _____

☐ _____

☐ _____

☐ _____

Mark	Explanation	Examples
¶	Begin a new paragraph. Indent the paragraph.	¶The boat finally arrived. It was two hours late.
∧	Add letters, words, or sentences.	My ∧best friend ate lunch with me t∧oday.
✗	Take out words, sentences, and punctuation marks. Correct spelling.	We ~~looked at and~~ admired the modd∕el airplanes.
≡	Change a small letter to a capital letter.	New York c̲i̲t̲y is exciting.
/	Change a capital letter to a small letter.	The F∕ireflies blinked in the dark.
⌄⌄ ⌄⌄	Add quotation marks.	⌄Where do you want the piano?⌄ asked the movers.
⌄,	Add a comma.	Carlton⌄, my cat⌄, has a mind of his own.
⊙	Add a period.	Put a period at the end of the sentence⊙
∽	Reverse letters or words.	Rae∽d carefully the instructions.
?	Add a question mark.	Should I put the mark here?
!	Add an exclamation mark.	Look out below!